Head
on the
Block

Head on the Block

Tony Cooper

Matador
9 Priory Business Park,
Wistow Road, Kibworth Beauchamp,
Leicestershire. LE8 0RX
Tel: (+44) 116 279 2299
Fax: (+44) 116 279 2277
Email: books@troubador.co.uk
Web: www.troubador.co.uk/matador

ISBN 978 1780884 448

British Library Cataloguing in Publication Data.
A catalogue record for this book is available from the British Library.

Typeset in 11pt Aldine401 BT Roman by Troubador Publishing Ltd, Leicester, UK

Matador is an imprint of Troubador Publishing Ltd

For me, this book marks the culmination of almost forty years in the teaching profession, over half of which I have spent as a headteacher. I would like to acknowledge and thank the very many people with whom I have had the pleasure of working during that time; they deserve full and sincere recognition for their professionalism and commitment to the education and welfare of young people. When I retired, I was proud to be leaving my school in the capable hands of all whom I knew would lead it to greater success and continue the dedicated hard work with which I have always associated them.

I also wish to thank my wife, Judith, who has read and re-read the many drafts of the text, making informed and helpful suggestions for improvement in both content and style. I thank her also, together with Simon and Becky, for having confidence in my ability to write and for providing continual encouragement for me to complete the book.

Tony Cooper

October 2012

Contents

Prelude — *1974*

For many people in Britain, 1974 was a memorable – if difficult – year. The election held in February resulted in the first hung parliament since 1929. Prime Minister Edward Heath had gone to the country hoping for a mandate to end the miners' dispute on his terms, but was narrowly defeated. After an abortive attempt to form a coalition with the Liberal Party, Heath resigned and Harold Wilson became Prime Minister for a second time, leading a minority Labour government.

Things were tough financially. Share prices collapsed, inflation was rampant and the basic rate of income tax was increased to 33%. Raising the highest tax-rate to over 80%, the Chancellor, Denis Healey, famously promised to squeeze the rich 'until the pips squeak'.

In 1974 Lord Lucan disappeared after the murder of his children's nanny, and twenty-one people were killed in the Birmingham pub bombings. China gave two giant pandas, Ching-Ching and Chia-Chia, to Britain, and the first McDonald's restaurant in the UK opened.

Manchester United were relegated from football's First Division.

And in 1974 I took up my first teaching post at a newly-opened comprehensive school in suburban west London.

The new establishment had been formed from two existing schools, one a secondary modern, the other a grammar school; the two buildings sat alongside each other, separated only by a shared playing field. These were interesting times. The school-leaving age had not long been raised from fifteen to sixteen. There were, therefore, cohorts of young people who no longer could enjoy the option of leaving school at the end of their fourth year of secondary education. There was now no choice: everyone was required by law to remain in school until the age of sixteen. Many students already stayed on to take O-levels, with the opportunity of continuing into the sixth-form. This was the expectation for most grammar-school students; it was not however the expectation of the majority of students in secondary modern schools.

The raising of the school-leaving age, affectionately known as RoSLA, had been a long time coming. In 1938, a report by the eminent academic Sir William Spens had recommended that young people should not leave full-time education before the age of sixteen. The Butler Education Act of 1944 raised the leaving age by one year to fifteen and decreed that it should be raised further, to sixteen, as soon as possible. It took almost 30 years for this be realised.

For the students I encountered in my first year of teaching, there was further change: they had endured the upheaval of their schools being reorganised to create a new, much larger, comprehensive school, complete with new name, new school uniform and a new headteacher. As part of the agreement to amalgamate the two schools, the former grammar and secondary modern students had retained their existing teaching groups and subject choices. This had created a distinct 'us and them' atmosphere – particularly amongst older pupils – and a certain lack of cohesion within the new institution.

Most of my work involved teaching GCE O-level and A-level students. However, I did have on my timetable a physics class of fifth-year students who fell very definitely into the RoSLA category, and for whom the Certificate of Secondary Education or CSE syllabus was my only resource. This qualification, introduced in 1965, was designed for students who were not thought sufficiently able to sit GCE, though it was not inherently different in content and was often referred to as simply a 'watered-down' O-level. It was certainly not appropriate for students who, if they had their way, would not be in school at all. Thus began a thrice-weekly – or should I say thrice-weakly? – battle with a group of recalcitrant fifteen year-olds who showed a distinct lack of interest in such concepts as specific heat capacity and Ohm's Law. 'What's the point of learning all this?' was their not infrequent battle-cry, to which I could only ever reply – under my breath – 'I haven't a bloody clue!'

Many schools required additional teaching space for the increased number of secondary-aged students. Hence, across the country, RoSLA buildings were especially shipped in and erected to accommodate this cohort of young people. Students then began to acquire the acronym as a badge of honour. 'We're the Rozlers!' a group once proudly announced to me as though, like Mods or Rockers before them, they regarded themselves as a distinct elite. Their use of the expression, however, left me unconvinced that they had any real appreciation of its literal meaning, but what was very clear was that they wished to stand out from the crowd. And they certainly did that.

There may have been RoSLA classrooms and RoSLA buildings for the RoSLA students, and in some schools specially appointed RoSLA teachers, but there appeared to me to be little by way of a RoSLA curriculum. In July 1974 the Member of Parliament for the Isle of Ely, one Clement Freud, brought to the House of Commons a private members' bill proposing an amendment to the new school-leaving age, to allow less academic pupils the chance to take up apprenticeships before their sixteenth birthday. Whilst acknowledging the money spent on additional school-rooms and buildings, Freud highlighted the lack of time or thought that had been devoted to trying to make the syllabus for these fifth-year students attractive. He had received many letters from teachers in his constituency who were bewildered as to what they should do with these youngsters. 'I took my 15 year-olds fishing, and it was a very rewarding exercise,' one teacher had written. 'We got on very well, but is this what was intended by the raising of the school-leaving age?'

Fortunately, the prospect of taking my RoSLAs even close to a river bank was never a serious consideration – only inevitable disaster lay in that direction – and in any case angling was not a hobby I had ever pursued, nor was it ever part of my teacher training. Instead I attempted to adapt the physics syllabus as best I could and struggled by with a mish-mash of pseudo-scientific experiments, using the poor quality apparatus and equipment not required for the more academic classes. The study of quantum mechanics at university had not prepared me for this. A faint glimmer of light at the end of a long dark tunnel was that some students – those whose birthdays fell early in the academic year – were allowed to leave after two terms, rather than having to stay through until the summer. Easter leavers, as they were known, were therefore excused the compulsion of the full extra year, though this made the study of a CSE course even less relevant, given that it led to an exam they would never take. I would sometimes, after a particularly disastrous lesson – anything involving gas, water or electricity was usually a fiasco – scan the list of birthdays to see if any of the most disengaged and disaffected had been born at the right time of year. The discovery that a particularly difficult or challenging student was an Easter leaver subsequently became a cause for genuine celebration.

But surely there were appropriate sanctions available to ensure co-operation of these RoSLA kids; wasn't corporal punishment still practised? Yes, corporal punishment was still employed in schools, right up until 1978, though it became rarely used in the immediately preceding years. In my second term of teaching, I was called to the deputy head's office to assist in the caning of a fifth-year boy whose crime I do not recall, but who had apparently deserved such punishment. I'm not sure what I had expected: a student proudly bending over to be hit on the backside, then thanking his assailant and shaking his hand before leaving the room with dignity and honour – if a little sore down below. But this was not Eton or Harrow. The student involved steadfastly refused to co-operate and accept his punishment with any sense of grace. It took three adults to hold the struggling boy down whilst the caning was executed, whereupon the victim ran from the room, expletives flying. He left behind in the room an atmosphere of shame which hung over us like an accusatory cloud; the humiliation had been ours, not his. That was to be my first – and thankfully last – experience of administering corporal punishment.

The headteacher of the school was a committed and hard-working professional with a passion for the welfare and education of her charges, but whose behaviour frequently bordered on the bizarre. I was one of nearly twenty newly-qualified teachers joining the school at that time. She fussed over us like a preparatory-school matron, insisting on us taking a hot meal at lunchtimes and, unbelievably, offering spoonfuls of cod-liver oil to anyone who looked to be, in her words, 'a little peaky'. Her public speaking became legendary and was frequently littered with inaccurate information, half-truths and, occasionally, downright fibs. One morning, an announcement was made at assembly of the success of the under-13 football team in reaching the Borough final by winning their match against another local school. The head complimented the team, telling the assembled students how she had watched much of the match from her office window and seen the winning goal. She praised the team for their achievement and spoke at length – a skill of all heads – of how proud she was of her pupils. Afterwards, one member of the team said to me, 'Sir, is the Head alright?' This was not an easy question to answer truthfully. 'What on earth can you mean?' I replied, to which he rejoined, 'It's just that the game was an away match!'

It was my particular misfortune to share a birthday with this poor woman. One morning in early February, whilst playing piano for assembly – I had unwisely ticked the box that appeared on application forms for teachers at the time: can you play the piano? – she leaned forward from the stage to announce to some three hundred children that she and I had something in common. 'What could it be?' we all thought. 'The same favourite television programme? A shared love of real ale? Support for the same football team?' Perhaps we were distantly related. Three hundred souls waited eagerly. 'Today is our birthday!' was the somewhat regal disclosure, 'Mr Koo-pah' – for that was how she pronounced my name – 'and I have a birthday today.' For one fearful moment I thought she was about to request my playing 'Happy Birthday' to accompany the assembled audience, even though by now, in my embarrassment, I had slunk down on the piano stool so far that my eyes were level with the keyboard. Instead she blew a kiss from the stage in my direction, and with that we departed, she to the sanctity of her office, and I to the relative security and sanity of the RoSLAs.

One of the longer-serving former grammar-school teachers who taught Latin – a guaranteed way of avoiding the RoSLA students was to be a teacher of Latin – frequently expressed his astonishment that anyone should be in the least surprised by the head's behaviour, dismissing her words and actions as completely in keeping with her vocation. 'All headteachers are mad,' he used to assert. 'They have to be to want to do the job in the first place.' In years to come I was to discover a certain grain of truth in this sentiment.

And so it was that – happily if naively – I completed my first year of teaching, secure in the knowledge that, whatever else might be my destiny, I would never, ever end up as a headteacher.

CHAPTER 1

Today

'It's seven o'clock on Monday the fourth of April. You are listening to Today on BBC Radio Four.'

Familiar words confirming the start of a working day. Today it's the first Monday of April, 2011 – Monday morning of the last week of term, the week before schools break up for the Easter holiday. It's been a long term; Christmas and New Year celebrations seem an age away. Now, at last, the mornings are lighter, and the early sun is well above the horizon by this time of day. The daffodils in bloom in front gardens and scattered in clumps by the roadside help lift the spirit. Although there is a freshness in the air, there's also an anticipation of the day's warmth to come after so many weeks of a particularly bitter winter.

For twenty-two years the start to my weekday mornings had followed an almost identical routine: a lengthy drive from my home to the school just outside Cambridge where I had been headteacher since 1989. Twenty-two years as headteacher – not far off a quarter of a century. Some heads have held their post for longer, but not many. During those years there had been much taking place in the world, most of which I had heard first on Radio Four. I remember hearing the breaking news of 9/11, the devastation caused by Hurricane Katrina, the space shuttle Columbia disaster, the conflict in Afghanistan and the death of Diana, Princess of Wales. Twenty-two years of disasters, natural and man-made. Twenty-two years of wars, earthquakes, floods and murders.

And twenty-two years of domestic politics. Over that time there had been five prime ministers and countless cabinet reshuffles. There had been eleven secretaries of state for education – that's an average of one every two years – each with their own distinct agenda, each with new ideas and initiatives, each bringing a change in educational policy which usually directly affected my work as a headteacher. As I turn onto the motorway, accelerating to merge with the speeding traffic, it is time for the business news. But company take-overs and profit warnings do not do much to hold my attention – I couldn't honestly say they ever did – and I find myself thinking instead of my week ahead.

Today I have a meeting with two students and their parents regarding an unpleasant situation which blew up on Friday afternoon. Things often blow up on a Friday, nicely in time for the weekend. Sometimes a period of two days away from school enables a degree of calming down to take place and gives me time to plan a considered response; other times it allows everyone to get even more worked up. People outside the profession have been known to tell me that dealing with awkward and difficult students must be time-consuming and stressful. As anyone within the profession – especially headteachers – will attest: dealing with troublesome students *is* time-consuming, but it's the awkward and difficult parents that are the real problem.

Mrs Smith's 15 year-old daughter had, during the lunch period, been on the receiving end of some hostile remarks from another girl. The daughter had retaliated, with language on both sides deteriorating more rapidly than the previous week's share prices. So far so good – or at least so capable of being resolved. By the end of the day however, both girls had managed to contact their respective mothers. Mrs Smith had taken it upon herself to arrive and wait outside the school in order to accost and verbally abuse her daughter's 'bully'. When news of this escalation had reached the other girl's mother – mobile phones can be such a mixed blessing – I had incurred a visit from this other, equally enraged, parent demanding instant retribution. With a few soothing words and the promise of a resolution on Monday, I had eventually managed to prise her out of my office, thereby allowing me to go home for the weekend. Both mothers were to see me this morning, intent on battling it out, each convinced of her own daughter's innocence and of the wrong that she had endured. Naturally it hadn't helped that one mum had rung the local authority to complain and the other had contacted a parent governor; most likely they'd phoned the News of the World – still then in circulation – and the Mail on Sunday as well. The local papers were also a good bet for a human interest, what-is-the-world-coming-to type of story enjoyed so avidly by their readers. Maybe there would be a call from an enthusiastic news-hound keen to get an exclusive. In the end of course, it will all have been the fault of the school and me in particular. I expect I will be to blame for the girls' misbehaviour in the first place. Probably I had invaded their human rights.

A lorry indicates to pull out into my lane and I flash my headlights to signify right of way, moving across to make space. I spot a police car up ahead and by instinct check the speedometer. The sports news, with results of Sunday's Premier League matches, has just registered on my consciousness, followed by an interview with a football manager hoping to avoid his team's end-of-season relegation. By the time we get to the racing tips – the 2.45 at Wetherby and the 3.15 at Huntingdon – my focus has switched again to consider another of the issues to be faced in the coming week: the school's financial situation.

Last week, schools received details of their budgets for the forthcoming year. As in so many years, the funding was insufficient to meet the current spending plans without the need for significant cuts. When schools were first given delegated budgets, with freedom to spend as they saw fit, the process was explained to me as follows: first set out all financial commitments for the year, take this away from the sum delegated, then prioritise the spending of the remaining sum according to the development plans of the school. That had been fine for a year or two until – with costs increasing more rapidly than income – the 'remaining sum' had become negative. Since then the process of setting the budget had been increasingly problematic. Some years were better than others; this year there were particular difficulties. Last September the school roll had fallen, only slightly, but none the less, fewer students meant less cash. Fair enough one might say but, in implementing an overall reduction of around 2%, it was a struggle to cut neatly from all commitments. Gas and electricity bills, for example, are difficult to reduce, given that the same number of classrooms still require heating. It was also hard to realise an equivalent reduction in cleaning costs, phone bills or many other services. And how does one cut 2% off an English teacher? Anyone can make savings of this order say the politicians, until it comes to their salaries or expenses. Salami slicing they call it; some years it seems more like full-scale butchery.

News headlines at half-past the hour: more Nato-led air operations over Libya, Gurkha redundancies announced, and criticism of proposed health service reforms puts pressure on the relevant minister. It's good to put my worries into some kind of perspective.

There are to be interviews later in the week for a senior position in the school. We have two excellent candidates but only one post to fill. Both teachers match the required criteria and both have the experience and expertise to do the job; it will be a very difficult decision. We have yet to finalise the composition of the interview panel, another task for today. I am very aware that I often agonise too deeply over this aspect of my role. Appointing staff from an interview process can be challenging at the best of times; having two good internal applicants is pleasing but it makes the selection process more difficult. Will there be anything other than cold comfort to offer the unsuccessful candidate?

Brake lights ahead; traffic slowing, soon to a standstill. The journey is seldom without hold-up: lorry broken down or shed its load, car accident or just a result of the sheer volume of traffic. I once calculated, when stuck in a jam and with little better to do, that in my 22 years I had driven over 350,000 miles on my journeys to and from school; that's equivalent to fifteen times around the Earth, or to the moon and halfway back, though not exactly at the speed of an Apollo spacecraft. On days with particularly bad traffic congestion I had contemplated the prospect of moving house to be closer to school, but I knew the disruption for my family would have been too high a price to pay.

'It's twenty to eight: time for a review of the newspapers,' says James Naughtie, always so carefully enunciating his words. That is apart from the time he mangled 'Jeremy Hunt the Culture Secretary' and, with an unfortunate spoonerism, shocked the entire nation with a four-letter word not usually heard at the family breakfast table. My attention is drawn to the précis of the morning's papers: headlines from the Times and the Guardian; an editorial comment from the Telegraph; a piece of rhetoric from the Daily Mail, neatly counterbalanced by a snippet from the Mirror.

There are a number of school policies to be reviewed this week. Policies are those documents which involve endless discussion and take countless hours to write; they also take hours to read, though few people seldom bother. One of my deputies, a woman not known for wasting words, had at times mischievously suggested cutting policy documents back to the bare bones. Thus a policy on attendance, currently running to twenty closely-typed sides of A4, might become simply: 'Students have to come to school.' The homework policy could be similarly slimmed down: 'Students must do their homework.' My favourite suggestion was for a policy on teaching and learning which schools had been recently requested to produce: 'Teachers teach and students learn.' What could be clearer? Sometimes there's a request from parents to see the school's behaviour policy, which perhaps might just have read: 'Students are expected to behave.' In my experience, people only usually asked to see a particular policy document prior to making a complaint; naturally we also had a complaints policy.

Every week brings fresh joys and headaches, often in equal proportion, though some days the joys seem few and far between. The term had started with burst water pipes, flooding the library and several classrooms. We had also experienced an overnight break-in with the consequent loss of many thousand pounds worth of computers; just as well our insurance premiums were paid up. There had also been some difficult issues with students and their families. On occasions, when a child suffered as the casualty of parental break-up, it seemed that the school was more a social service that an educational one – at times even a marriage guidance facility. A current concern involved a mother and father, recently separated, who had – over the past few weeks – played an elaborate game of ping-pong, with their son the unfortunate victim. They had steadfastly refused to communicate with each other, throwing all their angst in the direction of the school. Meanwhile the poor boy, already struggling with his education, was left increasingly confused and upset. I was fortunate in having staff who were extremely competent, and able to deal with such issues with great sensitivity and professionalism.

Last week there had been a student go missing overnight; fortunately she turned up the following morning, right as rain. Then there had been a boy who had taken inappropriate photos of his girlfriend; I will leave the meaning and use of the word 'inappropriate' to the reader's imagination. The pictures had unfortunately – but inevitably – found their way onto the internet and thereby available for all to see – more trouble ahead I predict. It doesn't seem to matter how much warning, advice and guidance is given regarding internet safety, there is always someone who thinks that a picture copied to just a few friends will remain discreet. Someone once told me that a secret can no longer be considered to be a secret once more than two people are told. That's my experience too.

'Thought for the Day' brings my attention back to the radio as I drive the last few miles to school. More familiar voices; will it be the Chief Rabbi today, perhaps Richard Harries, formerly Bishop of Oxford, or is it Anne Atkins? I have distinct preferences. This regular item in the Today schedule is known at the BBC as TftD. Google informs us that 'Terror from the Deep' also fits the acronym; critics of the three-minute pontification might think that more fitting, though I am not one of those. Besides, 'Thought for the Day' often provides inspiration for a morning assembly, especially when I am completely stuck for an idea. Tom Butler, Bishop of Southwark, has presented many interesting thoughts which have impressed me, including comments on leadership. 'Leaders produce followers,' he once told his listeners, 'but good leaders produce other leaders.' Rabbi Lionel Blue has made only infrequent appearances recently but he has popped up today. His TftDs always offer a good mix of spirituality and humour and usually conclude with a joke, often at his own expense or that of his religion. Today is no exception. He tells his listeners of a member of the wealthy Rothschild family who, visiting an East End street market, is offered cucumbers for sale at £10 each. Questioning the high price, 'Are cucumbers that rare around here?' he asks. 'No,' comes the reply, 'but Rothschilds are!' I'm not so sure how well that will work in assembly with Year Seven. Fortunately I already have something else prepared.

Not too bad a journey this morning, I think to myself, as I round the village green and pull into the school drive. Having found a parking space, locked the car and begun walking briskly towards the school's main entrance, briefcase in hand, one further thought flashes by me. Could I possibly have imagined, when I left as a pupil in 1970 that – over 40 years later – school would still be where I went to work every day?

CHAPTER 2

The Best Days of One's Life?

It was 1963 when I sat, and passed, the eleven-plus examination. Not that I had any deep understanding of the exam's significance other than the knowledge that, if I did well, I would go to my local grammar school. I had no real appreciation of the consequence of failing.

The eleven-plus was introduced as a result of the 1944 Butler Education Act and used to determine which type of school a pupil would attend for his or her secondary education. The tripartite system – as it became known – comprised grammar, secondary modern and technical schools, though the latter were very few in number. A handful of bilateral schools, which combined technical education with grammar or secondary modern schooling in a single institution, completed the picture. The proportion of children attending each type of school varied from one local authority to another but on average over three-quarters of children were in secondary modern schools and around twenty per cent were at grammar school. There was also a difference within authorities between the number of grammar school places available for boys and the equivalent number for girls. Local authorities were not required to provide equal number of places for each or indeed to set the same standards for entry; it was often harder for a girl to secure a grammar school place than for a boy.

In 1963 most children in their final year of primary school still took the eleven plus and transferred to selective schools. Two years later the Labour government issued a circular instructing local authorities to prepare for conversion to comprehensive education; this began the process of phasing out selective education in England and Wales. The Conservative government of the early seventies subsequently presided over a rapid growth in the number of comprehensive schools. Although the Secretary of State for Education, Margaret Thatcher, proceeded to rescind Labour's instruction, most local authorities had, by then, completed the conversion or were too committed to alter their plans. By 1975 the majority of authorities had dispensed with selection at eleven and more children were in non-selective than selective schools. A few counties such as Kent and Buckinghamshire retained their selection and continued to administer the eleven plus test; these authorities, and a scattering of others, have continued to preserve their grammar schools.

What were grammar schools like in the 1960's? How different an education did they provide from that of a typical comprehensive school forty years on? From personal experience the differences were considerable. At my grammar school, the teachers or masters – there were very few mistresses – all wore academic gowns, addressed their pupils by surname and required us to stand when they entered the classroom. Class teaching was almost exclusively didactic: much learning was by rote; many lessons involved copying from the blackboard; group work and discussion were virtually non-existent. It would be interesting to see how these grammar-school lessons might be judged against today's national inspection framework. There was, however, ample opportunity for experimental work in the sciences, which were taught as separate subjects. Practical woodwork lessons were also timetabled though, for the top stream, in the first year only. As might be expected, heavier emphasis was placed on academic subjects; Latin was taught to all and there were options to study Greek and ancient history, subjects which were especially popular in the sixth form.

Every four weeks or so during my first year at the school we were given a class order which ranked every boy in each form from top to bottom, based on marks awarded in individual subjects over the course of the month. It was a very crude assessment: on one occasion, with an overall mark of 94%, I came 21st out of the 25 boys in my class. The monthly order was delivered to the form by the headmaster personally who called each boy's name in turn, whereupon the individual stood to receive some form of acclamation or reprimand. We were named in strict order of attainment, commencing with the top boy in the class who received some semblance of praise. The praise became less effusive as the order progressed, and the comment became increasingly critical, irrespective of the mark achieved. Needless to say those at or near the bottom – including me on this occasion – received the sharpest tongue and the greatest loss of dignity. I was left very close to tears.

School life in the 1960s was different in so many ways. There was significantly more deference by pupils towards their teachers; conduct was more formal with less focus on the rights of individuals. Students were more accepting of the consequences of their actions and seldom complained to their parents who, if informed of a misdemeanour by their offspring, were more likely to reinforce the school's punishment than, as so often now happens, contact the school to remonstrate. Corporal punishment was administered from time to time by the headmaster or his deputy. There was also a degree of unofficial corporal punishment, actions by teachers which now would lead to instant dismissal. In PE, for example, it was not unknown for masters to use a slipper to physically admonish a pupil – a punishment which was never questioned or challenged. Prefects were allowed to refer boys to their own 'council', an unofficial court of law held in a basement common room – a part of the school never visited by teachers. Although I never experienced the misfortune to be called to prefects' council, there were many stories of pupils being ritually humiliated during these sessions and sometimes beaten.

Amongst the many teachers I recall was a maths master, an unfortunately large man with an equally unfortunate – if aptly descriptive – nickname. In order to preserve his energy he would, from time to time, ask a favoured student to leave school at break-time to buy cigarettes for him from the tobacconist across the road. Being requested to undertake this errand was viewed as a supreme honour and the escape from school, albeit brief, an enormous privilege. Equipped with the requisite cash – about two shillings – the twenty Park Drive would be duly purchased and delivered promptly to the door of the masters' room. The masters' room was situated at the end of a corridor, well apart from the mistresses' room which, being required to house the only three females on the teaching staff, was more akin to a broom-cupboard. On the few occasions that I had reason to visit the masters' room, I found it a most daunting experience. Pupils were not permitted to knock the door; it was necessary to wait for a master entering the room in order to make a particular request or enquiry. When the door was opened, the hapless student, quivering on the threshold of a forbidden territory, was engulfed in a dense cloud of tobacco smoke. Could one have imagined then, that fifty years on, it would be illegal for anyone to smoke anywhere inside a public building. As to the encouragement of minors to purchase tobacco products, that would today probably incur a custodial sentence, if not hasten the reintroduction of capital punishment.

But the most poisonous room in the school was, without doubt, the chemistry laboratory. There were two chemistry teachers at the school who, although occupying adjacent rooms, never appeared to speak to each other or communicate in any fashion. Each had his own class set of apparatus and equipment, jealously guarded and never, under any circumstance, loaned to the other. The elder of the two gentlemen, a man with part of one finger missing as a result of – it was commonly rumoured – a chemical explosion of his own making, was my teacher in the lower sixth-form. He was short on words and reluctant to offer much by way of explanation or theory, preferring instead a wholly practical approach to the subject, allowing us to mix chemicals in prodigious proportions; bucket chemistry it was sometimes called. Not for him the test-tube or the spatula but rather the largest flasks and beakers available, into which we shovelled mixtures and compounds by the lorry-load and poured liquids by the gallon. When the class prepared the gas nitrogen dioxide, the high ceiling of the pre-war building was rendered out of sight as a result of the vast clouds of the murky-brown, foul-smelling vapour. The gas was prepared by heating lead nitrate or by using copper to chemically reduce concentrated nitric acid, a liquid we slopped about in rather too haphazard a fashion than was good for us. No health and safety nonsense then, though a gas mask might have proved useful.

My least favourite subject was Latin with which I struggled doggedly through to the fifth year. Most Latin lessons consisted of translating aloud from the text, a paragraph at a time, one by one in class order. To avoid the embarrassment of displaying my level of grammatical ignorance and lack of vocabulary, it was essential to work out well ahead which part of the translation was likely to fall to me. It could then be prepared well in advance. When my turn had passed, I could switch off again until next time around – several weeks away. The only complication in this process came when the student due to read before me was unexpectedly absent or called away for some unknown reason, and his text came my way without warning. This then entailed the need to translate from scratch – a hesitant and mostly inaccurate process which led to much frustration, from my teacher as much as from me. Having scraped barely 20% in the January mock exam, I was not allowed to enter the O-level proper in the summer. There were no league tables then, but the headmaster relished announcing annually on Speech Day that the pass rate in all subjects was 100%. I was not given the opportunity to blemish that record; 20% in the mock was an unlikely indication of a pass in the real exam just a matter of a few months later. It was entirely my own fault. I had studiously learned the translation of much of the set text by heart but had regurgitated the wrong passage on my answer sheet.

Morning assembly was an extremely formal affair. Students entered the hall in silence as the deputy head glared coldly from the stage, fixing any boy who dared to risk a whisper to his neighbour with as evil an eye as he could muster. The stage, set with large table fronting three high-backed oak and leather chairs, was an emblem of authority which we looked up to in awe. The chair reserved for the headmaster was, naturally, the largest of the three. When all boys were seated, the duty prefect would, on a signal from the deputy, leave the hall to inform the head that his presence was due. The prefect would return and wait by the door until, after a few anticipatory minutes – timed I suspect to give increased importance to the arrival, like a congregation's wait for the bride – the head swept in as we all stood to our feet. Gown flapping, he would mount the steps to his chair centre-stage, giving the command, 'Sit down boys.'

This daily ceremony consisted of a passage from the Bible – read by the prefect – and a hymn sung by all, though little could ever be heard above the organ. I think the staff in particular were well-practised in the ability to move their lips without actually singing a note. There then followed a short prayer delivered by the head, and the Lord's Prayer garbled by the assembled body at such speed as to make it virtually meaningless. The whole affair was spiritually vacuous, though undoubtedly it fulfilled the legal requirement for all schools to hold a daily act of worship. After being seated again, the boys who had been excused from taking part for religious reasons, being Roman Catholics or perhaps Jehovah's Witnesses – we never knew – were allowed to enter to hear the notices for the day. We then stood again as the head hurried back to the comfort and peace of his study – a study not an office, as most headteachers' rooms are now called – an indication of the role being more academic and less managerial than is the case today.

I enjoyed my time at grammar school, making a number of good friends, some of whom I have remained in contact with for over forty years. I was basically a diligent, hard-working and well-behaved student though there were some occasional lapses in conduct... During the midday break, sixth-formers were allowed out of school. Usually we drifted around the town for the duration, buying cakes and buns from the bakers or visiting the record shop to thumb through the LP selection and peruse the covers of the latest Rolling Stones or Motown releases. On the occasion of my seventeenth birthday, my friends and I dispensed with the usual routine and celebrated the big day with beer and sandwiches in a high-street pub. Unfortunately it occurred that I had more beer than sandwiches. Even if the teacher of my afternoon double physics lesson didn't query the smell of alcohol on my breath or the rather glazed look in my eyes, he must have been suspicious of my need to visit the toilet three times in the space of just over an hour. But there was no repercussion or recrimination; amazingly I got away with it.

It is difficult to imagine what occupied headteachers during the sixties and seventies. There was no Ofsted – the Office for Standards in Education, no publication of inspection findings or examination results, indeed little public accountability at all. There was no statutory performance management or any apparent formal assessment of teachers, no criteria for grading teaching, and no

National Curriculum, whose time did not come around for more than twenty years. The school curriculum was the preserve almost exclusively of teachers and rarely changed; government involvement was virtually non-existent. There was little by way of health and safety legislation or any statutorily-required school policies. Governors' meetings were far less frequent than now, with none of the numerous sub-committees currently enjoyed (or endured!) Schools did not have devolved budgets and consequently had little control over spending; officers of the local authorities were responsible for most financial decisions now taken by heads. It was the local authority who sent round their employees to make any required minor repairs, the local authority who appointed supply teachers to cover staff absence, and the local authority who made the decision on such matters as when the school's heating could be turned on – at the beginning of October – and off again – at the end of April.

Teachers' lives must also have been considerably less stressful. There were no routine inspections or observations of classroom practice. Annual reports for students were far less comprehensive or informative than now, and frequently consisted of one word or phrase for each subject. 'Satisfactory' was the most common expression – we shall come to see that this no longer means what it did then – and 'Good' if you were lucky. The words were sometimes embellished by the addition of 'very'. I had 'excellent' once or twice on my reports, though never for Latin. There were no parental consultation meetings, no careers events or university information sessions. My parents never crossed the school threshold, not because they had never wanted to, but because there had never been an invitation for them to. The school was the territory of the staff: parents keep out! After school hours, at weekends and during holidays, the site was locked and bolted. There was no conception of the building ever being open for the benefit of the wider community.

I cannot say however – despite the degree of indifferent teaching – that my grammar school served me badly. I gained a good set of O-level and A-level results, sufficient to gain entry to my first choice of university and embark upon what was to become my eventual career. Most teachers were benign, some even friendly and, though very much out of the 'old school' mould, most usually had the best interests of their pupils at heart.

And so it was that, in my last ever school assembly, I sang the end of term hymn *Lord dismiss us with thy blessing* for the final time, and my days as a schoolboy were over.

CHAPTER 3

Physics is Fun

My A-level success led me to a physics degree course at a college, then part of the University of London, which was highly respected for science and engineering. To say that I found the work difficult over the ensuing three years would be, by any standard, an extreme understatement. I was one of two hundred first-year physics undergraduates, many of whom – though sufficiently able – had chosen not to apply to Oxford or Cambridge, or had missed a place there by a whisker. I appreciated within days that I was below the average ability of the cohort, certainly not within the range of students likely to gain a first or second class degree. Consequently, I set about what was to be a long slog towards third class honours. Recent government pronouncements have suggested that such a class of degree could, in future, bar an individual from gaining qualified teacher status; legislation may well follow. Had there been such regulation in the 1970s, I would never have been able even to enter the teaching profession, let alone achieve a headship. I have sometimes considered the thought that I might have come down from university with a higher class of degree had I chosen, dare I say, a 'softer' subject at a less prestigious institution.

But physics it was, and I did not find it easy. For a start I was younger than most other students, having been accelerated through secondary school by a year, a move that, in retrospect, may not have been entirely to my advantage. I was also handicapped by having taken only a single A level in maths – almost all other undergraduates had taken a second, further mathematics course. In addition to the daily lectures, held in the comparatively modern physics department building, we had two hours of maths every morning in a cavernous, nineteenth-century lecture hall which is now – appropriately – part of the Victoria and Albert Museum. There were also afternoons spent in the physics laboratory, and a weekly group tutorial. We did not pay tuition fees in 1970 but, had we done so, there could have been no cause for complaint about value for money. The more modest provision of lectures and tutorials for many non-science courses at other universities might not have stood up to the same claim.

Despite the difficulty of the work, there were many pleasurable hours spent making friends, socialising in the union bar and drinking coffee until the early hours. There was a variety of clubs and societies offering a wide range of activities, and the West End cinema was just a pre-decimal sixpenny underground journey away. I also enjoyed several weekends out of London, climbing and walking with the college mountaineering club which I had joined in my first term.

There were also a few calamities. In 1972, during a rag-week stunt (do universities still have rag weeks?) outside a pub in the Tottenham Court Road, I failed to respond quickly enough to a request from a uniformed officer of the Metropolitan Police to 'move along'. The request, it transpired, was more an instruction than a polite invitation and my hesitation resulted in a charge of obstructing the said officer 'in the execution of his duty'. After an hour or more in the cells and a long walk home – there being then no all-night bus service – I appeared the next day to face the charge in court. The magistrate was neither impressed by, nor sympathetic to, the rag-week antics of long-haired left-wing students and I was duly fined five shillings, or 25 pence in the soon-to-be-introduced new money. There had been a number of other students found similarly guilty on that night; many of us were aggrieved by the police action, which we felt to have been more heavy-handed than was necessary to keep the peace. The organiser of our rag committee subsequently contacted the president of the National Union of Students, a man who later became a Member of Parliament and Home Secretary in the Blair government, to assist in lodging a complaint. As should have been realistically expected, this action came to nought; we were received with consideration and given a polite reception but little by way of practical support. Despite several extensive searches by the Criminal Records Bureau in recent times, this record of mine has remained suitably buried.

There was another escapade which, had I been apprehended, might well have become an addition to this record. As a member of the College's mountaineering club I found myself drawn to the challenge of climbing a prestigious Crown monument which overlooked the Royal Albert Hall. This challenge had been part of the club's folk-lore for many years, a test of skill and daring and, one might add, a student antic of sheer foolishness. Having decided to undertake this particular stunt, and persuaded an initially reluctant fellow climber to accompany me, I set out enthusiastically late one November evening to accomplish my goal. After a quite difficult ascent involving tape slings and running belays with my assistant holding the ropes below, I managed to reach my summit. The subsequent descent involved an abseil using a tape loop through which ran the rope, the whole apparatus being theoretically recoverable from ground level. But it was not to be; the rope came away easily enough but managed to leave behind the tape clinging stubbornly to the apex of the monument. The next morning I revisited the site of my transgression to witness the vivid pink, tell-tale piece of equipment fluttering disturbingly in the autumn breeze, informing the world that the edifice to which it was attached had been irreverently violated. A few days later I noticed that it had disappeared. Divine intervention perhaps? Had there been an undercover operation by the SAS, or was it retrieved by an unknown fellow mountaineer? To this day the mystery remains unsolved.

Meanwhile there was plenty of physics to get on with. Although no one would doubt their scientific knowledge or expertise, my lecturers and tutors varied considerably in their teaching ability. I have often thought that, for some unhappy individuals, the knowledge of one's academic subject, and the ability to teach it, are in some kind of inverse proportion. I am convinced that my own teaching, particularly the ability to explain mathematical and physical concepts, benefited from earlier struggles to comprehend the subject material.

One course of note was held in a lecture theatre which was patently not large enough to accommodate the entire year group. We were told by the lecturer however, as he began the first of his poorly-delivered presentations, not to worry since an anticipated drop-off in attendance would mean there would, in later weeks, be seats for all. He was quite correct. That first week students were sitting on steps in the aisles and crammed two to a seat on the back rows. The second week saw an improvement with almost enough places for everyone. I cannot speak for subsequent weeks since, having gained very little from the first two sessions, I assisted personally with the overcrowding situation by joining the ranks of those making their notes from the recommended text-book as an alternative to attending the lectures.

Although we did not have to pay tuition fees, and the student grant was sufficient – just – to cover term-time living expenses, there was still a need for paid employment during the university vacations. I worked variously as a barman, a security guard and night watchman, and as a porter in a hospital operating theatre. Bar work was enjoyable, with its own after-hours rewards, and the time passed quickly. As a security guard and night watchman, the exact opposite was the case; the uniform was smart but no compensation for the seemingly endless drudgery of a twelve-hour shift. Hospital portering was by far the most rewarding and the best paid of all my holiday jobs, though it never led me to consider that I might have made a career for myself in medicine.

In my third year of university I shared – with three other students – a flat just off the Edgware Road, a stone's throw from Marble Arch. The morning walk to college, across Hyde Park and through Kensington Gardens was delightful. I enjoyed the changing seasons, from the first signs of autumn at the start of the academic year in September, through the winter and spring months to the summer exam season. Returning late in the evening, when the parks were closed, involved a circuitous bus-ride, several stops on the Circle Line or – far quicker and cheaper – a clamber over the park railings – yet further illegal activity in all probability.

My flat was adjacent to the national office for teacher recruitment and, purely out of passing interest, I called in one morning to investigate the possibility of enrolling on a post-graduate degree course. I learned that a further fully-funded year of university could lead to the opportunity of becoming a teacher, new regulations having been just enacted to make a post-graduate teacher training qualification compulsory. Until then the possession of a university degree alone had conferred qualified teacher status, explaining perhaps why many schools were staffed by highly academic individuals who had never mastered the craft of the classroom.

Having endured the pressure of formal exams every June for as long as I could remember – my finals were without doubt the most stressful experience ever – I was adamant that, on graduating, I would find a teacher training course which was assessed practically and continuously rather than by written examination. I found exactly what I wanted at a red-brick university in the Midlands. The course, which I started in September 1973, involved two lengthy periods of teaching practice and a minimum of theory and lectures. This was just perfect.

My first outing to the classroom was at a large comprehensive school on the outskirts of a market town some ten miles from my university school of education. From the first day I knew I had made the right decision to enter teaching and felt comfortable in the classroom where I enjoyed teaching physics to students of varying ages and abilities. That was not to say that some classes weren't challenging, but I received excellent support from my head of department and other colleagues in the science faculty. The school was calm, the staff dedicated and enthusiastic, and I was made to feel extremely welcome. Some things went wrong of course, but the environment was such that mistakes were accepted as an inevitable part of the development of any new teacher in training; there was no culture of blame. The school was in an authority that had enjoyed a comprehensive system of secondary education for many years and was well established and respected within its local community.

My second teaching practice proved to be far more of an undertaking. I embarked on an eight-week placement in a boys' secondary modern school, in an authority which had – unlike its rural counterpart – retained selection at eleven and kept its bipartite system of secondary education. The school was led by a short, stout Welshman with a voice and temper that were legendary. It was not only the schoolboys who were intimidated by this all-powerful oligarch; more than once I found myself suitably cowed by his explosive tantrums and shouts from afar, having mistakenly interpreted them to be aimed at me.

The school was rigidly streamed, with six classes in each year group. One of my classes was 5F which constituted a group of boys at the lowest possible end of the ability spectrum. And didn't they know it. They had survived almost five years in the bottom set as it moved relentlessly through the school. An occasional boy had escaped by promotion to 5E – an accomplishment only dreamed of by others. The students were remarkably well behaved given that they had endured an educational diet consisting, as far as I could ascertain, of copying work from the blackboard and colouring pictures for display on the classroom wall. We proceeded to battle our way through a variety of elementary science experiments. The timetable heralded the subject I was designated to teach as 'general science', euphemistically named to disguise the fact that individual science subjects were thought too taxing for pupils of this ability. There was no biology involved during the term I was with the class (thankfully), but I was able to mix a little chemistry in with what was predominantly physics, in order to provide more varied entertainment for the students. They watched me switch on a vacuum pump to suck the air from a large glass flask containing an electric bell. With the air in the flask the bell could be heard loud and clear. With the air extracted, the bell, though still seen to be vibrating, could not be heard, proving that – as any schoolchild knows – air is needed in order for sound to travel. Except that the experiment didn't work. The pump was singularly inefficient, the flask only partly evacuated, and I was only able to confirm this fundamental law of physics by speaking quietly when the air was present and raising my voice to cover the ringing sound when the jar was supposedly airless. School science was once described to me thus: if it grows or moves it's biology; if it smells or explodes it's chemistry; and if it doesn't work it's physics.

We had better luck with lenses and mirrors – though the rate of breakage was alarming – and we connected small light bulbs to power sources capable of delivering ten times the required voltage, with the inevitable result that they too joined the school's ever lengthening list of broken or dysfunctional equipment. We put sodium into water – an experiment which could now get teachers struck off – and played with globules of mercury on an asbestos mat – ditto. Such niceties as safety goggles and screens were not available, and assessment of risk was minimal. Making nitrogen dioxide produced great excitement as the dense brown fumes took over and filled the laboratory – just as in my own school days – until the far end of the room was no longer visible and students were left coughing and choking in a heap on the floor.

The school's staff room might have fallen straight from the pages of fiction, Evelyn Waugh's *Decline and Fall* perhaps or maybe the Beano's *Bash Street Kids*. An ill-assorted collection of old-fashioned armchairs, many – like the staff themselves – showing their age and stuffing, were positioned around three sides of this cold, inhospitable room. On the fourth side, adjacent to the door, were a sink and a table hosting an array of mostly unwashed cups and mugs. An aged kettle and fridge completed the catering arrangements. Although they bore no visible signs of labelling, it was immediately obvious to any casual observer that the chairs were allocated to regular users. On the rare occasions I visited the staff room, I chose a seat with deliberate caution and always sat in anticipation of having to vacate my pew to its rightful owner. Nearly all the staff appeared to be habitual smokers, and although not quite as toxic as my gas-filled classroom, the tobacco fumes replaced what little air was otherwise available for breathing. In the middle of the room stood a three-quarter sized snooker table with torn baize, two cues minus their tips and an incomplete set of coloured balls. I never saw the table in use.

But I successfully survived this austere environment and even discovered that my enthusiasm for a career in teaching had sharpened. I bade a fond farewell to the lively characters of 5F, and a less-heartfelt goodbye to the Welshman – whom I suspect had never known who I was. I passed both my teaching practices comfortably, my school mentors pleased with my performance in the classroom. My essays were judged passable – solidly satisfactory, though not overtly commendable – and I emerged in the summer of 1974 as a fully-qualified member of the teaching profession.

CHAPTER 4

The Road to the Top

Having successfully completed my first years of teaching – and survived the RoSLAs intact – I had decided by 1979 to seek a new challenge. The spring of that year found me at a large comprehensive community school in the shadow of Heathrow Airport as head of a physics department of three teachers. The school in its present location had been open for only four years, having been built to replace a nearby older establishment. Full double-glazing kept aircraft noise at bay, though we were not directly below either of the eastern landing approaches. Even with a change in wind direction – which led to planes taking off towards the school – a local agreement prevented the use of the northern runway – thereby avoiding air traffic immediately overhead. Only Concorde caused other than the slightest disturbance.

In May of that year, Margaret Thatcher became Prime Minister. Jim Callaghan had clung to power throughout the winter of discontent, so called because of public sector industrial action by – amongst others – water workers, ambulance drivers and refuse collectors. His majority in the Commons, never above single figures, had shrunk to zero; only a pact with the Liberal Party and, later, the Scottish Nationalists had enabled him to govern. In March of the New Year Callaghan lost a motion of confidence, by a single vote, triggering a general election in which his party was defeated. The new Conservative government set about its well-publicised task of restoring economic stability and curbing the power of the unions. 'Where there is discord may we bring harmony,' asserted Mrs. Thatcher from the steps of Number 10, quoting Saint Francis of Assisi. With that she set about her mission to reduce inflation, which was running at 27%, and to resolve the industrial strife in her own, now legendary, fashion.

My new school had a lively and eclectic mix of staff. In common with many schools at the time, it had only just started to admit a comprehensive intake of students, and had taken a while to adjust. The teachers who had spent most of their careers in the secondary modern school had been complemented by an intake of younger, more recently qualified staff. It was an extremely forward-looking establishment enjoying, for the most part, well-motivated, friendly students, eager to learn. Built to serve the community, the school was open from early morning until late evening – seven days a week – and offered exceptional facilities for education, recreation and leisure.

It was here that I developed an understanding of community education and an insight into the immense potential of opening up school buildings for wider use. Although less than ten years since I had left my grammar school, it was hard not to be struck by the complete contrast between my alma mater and the school where I now found myself teaching. The London borough under whose authority the school functioned had, like some other local authorities across the country, begun to fully embrace the concept of community education and build new schools to serve the public at large.

The largely Asian population within the school's catchment area was extremely ambitious. Valuing education as the means to a good career, parents were desperate for their children to succeed. The less academic subjects and options were viewed with substantial disdain, the Certificate of Secondary Education (CSE) being considered significantly inferior to the GCE O-level, even though a top grade at CSE was deemed equivalent to an O-level pass. Many students wished to become doctors. For some this was an entirely realistic ambition: these students were frequently successful in securing places at medical school. Sadly, for the young people who were less academic, ambition often exceeded ability. In the sixth form, students who did not secure the requisite number of CSEs or O-levels to embark upon an A-level course of study satisfied themselves by re-sitting their previous year's examinations. As had become very apparent in most schools, students retaking their O-levels rarely improved their grades and in some cases performed less well. On offer, therefore, was a range of less academic courses, recently introduced to enable students to progress – sometimes to higher education – but through a more vocational route. This approach was not always acceptable to students, even less so to their parents. On more than one occasion it transpired that a father believed his son or daughter to be taking a higher level course than was actually the case. This led to many misunderstandings and was the cause of much stress to the young people involved. Similarly, for many, university was the only acceptable long-term goal. The polytechnics, which ironically have all since gained their own university status, were not seen at the time as suitable destinations.

After two enjoyable and fulfilling years as head of the physics department within a larger science team, an opportunity came up for me to apply for the post of head of sixth form and become part of senior management. At the comparatively young age of 28, my application was considered by some within the school's hierarchy as precocious and a demonstration of inflated ambition. That was not however – fortunately for me – the view of the headteacher who, newly in post following the retirement of her predecessor, appointed me to the position. There followed several years of engaging and rewarding work, with greatly enhanced responsibility including a short spell as deputy head, caused by the secondment of the head and the consequent temporary promotion of one of her deputies.

There was also much fun. The staff were a lively bunch who worked hard but knew how to enjoy themselves. End of term parties were legendary; there were social nights out and weekend staff trips – the Saturday cruise to Calais was a favourite. We also took part in annual end-of-the-pier style song and dance shows, performances which were a highlight of the year and provided a very agreeable way of winding down at the end of term. For many weeks we would practise music-hall medleys and sing and dance our way through three nightly performances in front of a paying audience – the audience paying us that is, not the other way round. My hitherto well-hidden skills (?) as an amateur magician were harnessed and I was persuaded to swallow razor blades, burn and restore pound notes and produce the proverbial (fake) rabbit from a hat. Tommy Cooper, almost but not quite my namesake, had long been one of my heroes and, though not exactly the London Palladium, I did enjoy being on the stage.

It was during these years that I undertook a part-time higher degree: a Master's in education or MA. This was not easily embarked upon. Most universities and colleges of education insisted that applicants for further study possessed at least a second class honours degree, ideally a 2:1. My paltry third class affair made me strictly ineligible. On one occasion I was invited to lead a session about some of my recent work as head of sixth form – there had been some interesting curriculum developments at the school in which I had been involved – to a group of mature students on an MA course for which I had been turned down. I could not avoid drawing the audience's attention to the irony of my being qualified to teach on the course but not qualified to attend as a student. Not prepared to give up on the prospect of a higher degree, I did manage – after several rejections – to be accepted for a Master's at a relatively obscure institution. This lesser-known college has since merged with a lesser less-known college, which in turn has now merged with one of the most established constituent colleges of the University of London. So there!

My short spell as an acting deputy had convinced me that I should seek a permanent deputy headship and, in 1985, I set about applying in earnest for such a position. Unlike Samuel Johnson, I had become somewhat tired of London – or at least its suburbs – and was ready for a move away from the metropolis. The post which I eventually acquired – after a few false starts – was in a large comprehensive school in one of the new townships in the expanded Greater Peterborough. The school was an integral part of its surroundings and epitomised the ideal of the community school. There were facilities shared with the public at large, such as the library, which functioned as a dual resource, and a swimming pool open at weekends and in the school holidays. As the school had grown, it had attracted a collection of enthusiastic and forward-looking teachers. There were many innovative curricular initiatives, most of which were highly beneficial to students and often of local and national significance. We were all encouraged to work in teams, developing and promoting the very best in pupil-centred education. This was a highly progressive school, not progressive in the trendy, anything-goes sense so rightly derided by politicians and the press, but in the manner of creative and professional development, questioning current practice, continuously seeking improvement and wanting at all times to provide the very best education and care for students. Initiatives came thick and fast and it was not always easy to keep up. Occasionally, my role as deputy head was to act as a brake on developments in order to ensure that one significant change was fully embedded before the next one came along.

The school was led by an extremely charismatic man for whom an eight-hour day would have meant merely part-time working. He was at his desk by seven each morning and – if he did leave before six – it was usually to return later for an evening meeting. He was a highly principled head, under whom I was proud to have worked, and from whom I learned a great deal. There were, very occasionally, times when the other deputies and I thought he might have been a little out of step on a particular issue, but a subtle word from us was usually appreciated and would always do the trick. I later came to value my deputies doing the same for me when they thought I was about to approach a situation unwisely, make a poor decision, or simply continue digging myself into an ever-deepening hole.

These were the years of Sir Keith Joseph and Kenneth Baker at the Department of Education. The National Curriculum was forged, testing at the ages of four, seven, eleven and fourteen was introduced and teachers' pay and conditions were changed for ever. We had work-time directives and new contracts. The teachers' year was lengthened and staff training days came into being – Baker days as they were known – a label which stuck for many years. It was during this time that education moved up the national agenda and the involvement of Whitehall and Westminster in school structure and curriculum heightened significantly. Politicians were sharpening their knives.

I cannot overstate the learning that took place during my time as a deputy. My greatest sadness was that, in the years after I had moved on, although the school remained highly successful, the demand for school places in the area fell dramatically. The local population aged; children grew up and moved away with no influx of younger families to replace them. By 2007 numbers had fallen sufficiently for the local authority to sanction amalgamation with another local school in a new building on a different site. In 2009 the school, although by then only thirty years old, was demolished to make way for a cut-price supermarket. So now, where my office once stood, runner beans and potatoes are packaged and awaiting purchase, pineapples are two for a pound, and packs of tomatoes are buy-one-get-one-free. Where I taught science, cans of beer, cider and lager are stacked floor to ceiling, and the former music studios now house giant refrigerators selling butter, cheese and milk. Such is progress.

For many deputy heads, the role is not considered to be the pinnacle of their career. The desire for even greater responsibility and the wish to lead a school outweigh all other considerations; the top job is what they aspire to. After three years as a deputy, I too came to the conclusion that headship was what I sought and, in 1989, after a few unsuccessful applications – close on one occasion, light years away on others – I was appointed to the post I went on to hold for 22 years. I became a headteacher.

CHAPTER 5

The Art of Headship

Headteachers come in all shapes and sizes, with many different personalities and temperaments. Some are friendly, sociable and liberal, others detached, unapproachable and authoritarian, though I am pleased to say that the former outweigh the latter in number. They run their different schools in a myriad different ways, endeavouring to retain their sanity but not always managing to achieve this. Many heads are held in high regard, respected and looked up to by teachers and pupils; others less so, and perhaps with good reason. I always strived to gain the confidence of my staff and students through honesty, fairness and hearty doses of plain common-sense, but am not convinced that I was always successful.

A sense of humour helped too. Being able to laugh, especially at oneself, is a healthy and helpful mechanism for bringing people on side – it is hard not to find some amusement in most situations. I have a perpetual view that many heads cannot always enjoy the lighter aspects of their role and take themselves far too seriously. During a difficult meeting between me, one of my deputies and an extremely truculent year 11 girl, I came within an inch of completely losing my temper, my blood pressure rising above the top of the Richter Scale. At a critical moment, after we had reached a solid impasse, the girl shouted at us both, swore loudly and stormed out of the room – flounced would be too weak a descriptor – slamming the door so hard it brought a picture off the wall. As it fell to the floor, shattering the glass into a million pieces across the carpet, there was a second's stunned silence before my deputy rescued me from near apoplexy and a potential heart-attack. Seeing the amusing side of the situation in an instant, she burst out laughing. And it was funny. Two grown-up professionals completely wrong-footed by a fifteen year-old and with little more to show for our efforts than a sea of broken glass. Laugher was infinitely preferable to either anger or tears, the only other potential responses I could have mustered. What could I do but laugh too?

There is no handbook or A to Z guide for headteachers. When I took up my post, the National Professional Qualification for Headteachers (NPQH) – a substantial and rigorous training course for aspiring heads – had yet to be introduced. It is currently not possible to be appointed to headship without this qualification, though I wonder how many good people have been put off from seeking the top job because of this necessary prerequisite. Some heads place the letters NPQH delicately after their name – I believe it should go between the PhD and the OBE – though I'm not completely certain it achieves the aim of enhancing their status. It appears that the scope of this qualification may be amended at some point in the future, and become no longer essential.

I was brought up instead on self-help and the support of colleagues and fellow headteachers. As part of my quest for self-improvement, I discovered a short book on successful leadership which was both enlightening and helpful. Although written for a more commercial market than education, *The One Minute Manager* provided valuable advice for fledgling headteachers like me. Over time I learned to adopt the One Minute Manager's positive strategies for personnel management and leadership. The world did not always reciprocate however; I grew accustomed to bracing myself for the brickbats that came when I had mishandled a situation, and learned to expect little positive feedback when things were going well.

On taking up my headship, I inherited from my predecessor a booklet of uncertain vintage, though its price of five shillings, printed on the back cover, gave some clue to its ancestry. *Some problems of Headmasters* offered a fascinating insight into the world of school leadership in previous millennia. Note that heads were presumed to be men. There were, I am sure, plenty of headmistresses around at the time but I assume that – unlike their male counterparts – they never suffered problems. The booklet was arranged into chapters, crisply headed: pupils, parents, staff and so forth, each category presenting its own particular set of potential disasters. Amongst other nuggets of information, the author gave advice on the wearing of academic gowns, the most efficient use of corporal punishment and the importance of a well-ordered stationery cupboard. The latter he regarded as requiring the designation of a member of teaching staff who would be given extra free periods and the payment of an additional allowance for such weighty and serious responsibility. This responsibility, it was affirmed, was a substantial stepping-stone on the path to a deputy headship. The same booklet, in a sure sign of its time, gave advice to heads on dealing with a pupil complaining that his teacher has been overtly physical in reprimanding him. 'The way you have been treated may not have been right,' suggests an appropriate response to the student, 'but you don't seem to have suffered any great harm, and you did deserve some punishment didn't you? Isn't it a bit your fault if Mr X became angry and hit you?'

The art of headship has developed considerably since then though, as I discovered in my early years of teaching, there was some unconventional practice around. I once worked for a headteacher who took it upon himself, on the last working day of every month, to tour the school, individually handing teachers their payslips. It was as though he regarded himself as paymaster, personally responsible for remunerating his staff, presumably under the misguided assumption that they would be grateful to him. They weren't. These outings represented the few times he was seen away from the office where he spent much of his day, hiding behind a set of 'traffic lights' mounted alongside the door to indicate whether a visitor might enter, wait or just give up and go away. The light was invariably red. Someone once told me of a headteacher with such a contraption which had never shown the green light, for the simple reason that the bulb had blown and not been replaced. Perhaps he had switched the device to green with such enthusiasm that the surge of current had seen the better of the tiny filament. Whatever the cause, this was a sure-fire way to keep away unwanted interruption and unwelcome callers.

I have also worked for heads with a much more open-door approach, welcoming all visitors, staff and students throughout the day. One in particular was a great inspiration and, with his unending enthusiasm and positive attitude, helped me to become a modestly successful headteacher. 'Students come first,' he once told me. 'Staff come second. Everything else comes a very poor third.' I cannot see how that philosophy could ever have been realised with a red light shining continuously outside the door.

Headteachers, I have observed, are extremely adept at being able to speak in public, often at short notice, on any subject, although it must be appreciated that this can sometimes be at the expense of saying much of significance. By the time one has told the audience the importance of what they are about to hear, most people will have already switched off. Having then delivered the substance of the message, the whole thing can be wrapped up by re-enforcing what has just been told – men and women of the clergy are also good at this technique; I think of it, like any sermon, as a kind of verbal sandwich. This is also a sure-fire approach to leading school assemblies, as it can be used to pad out a short message to any required length. I once gave an assembly to a group of students who, it later turned out, had suffered the same text being read to them by their head of year the previous week. Not a single person – student or member of staff – brought this to my attention; I only discovered the error of duplication by chance. Was it out of deference that no-one informed me of the repetition or was it, more likely, that nobody had noticed because they had simply not been listening?

From time to time headteachers enjoy a well-deserved break from school routine in order to attend a course or conference. Such events provide an opportunity for reflection and the chance to explore and discuss educational matters and priorities with fellow school leaders. But there is nothing more calculated to raise alarm amongst teachers and senior managers than a head who has just returned from such an away-day bursting with new ideas. 'Oh dear,' was the usual response – seen on faces, if not actually spoken – when, back in school after such an event, I announced that I had come up with a brilliant new initiative. It is said that headteachers are always having new ideas – that's what they do. New ideas are always needed – even if seldom appreciated – and must be launched before the last new idea has had an opportunity to make any real progress. New ideas are what prevent heads from having to follow through old ideas. In most schools, it is the role of the deputy heads to restrain headteachers from launching too many of their latest fads onto an undeserving staff, and consequently allowing heads to make total fools of themselves by introducing changes which would be completely unworkable. Any one or more of a range of strategies can be successfully employed by loyal deputies in order to deflect, subvert or, if necessary, completely scupper any proposed new wheeze from their boss:

1 Heap praise upon the head for the excellent new idea, make clear that it is well-worthy of implementation, but then do nothing about it. Most heads are flattered to be listened to and to have their ideas appreciated and accepted, although in all probability many are not original but have come from a speaker at their last conference – or worse, from an educational text. (Beware heads who read too many books on education.) With any luck, by the following week, the head will be on to his or her next initiative, having assumed that the original had been put into practice, or having forgotten all about it.

2 Suggest that the proposal is so brilliant and important that it should be put to the governing body. This would then require discussion at the relevant sub-committee before appearing as an agenda item at the full governors' meeting. By this means, many weeks – if not months – can elapse before the issue again sees the light of day, by which time everybody will have moved on to something new. The advantage of this tactic is that there is never any need either to approve or to reject the initiative.

3 Set up a working party, meeting half-termly or preferably less frequently, before reporting back with a final recommendation. Given that the outcome of the working group may require ratification by the governing body, this approach has the added benefit of employing the addition of the previous strategy. It is quite possible for a full year to pass whilst this process is engaged, and is similar to governmental use of an official enquiry, which buys valuable time, and can even postpone potentially difficult decisions until after the next general election.

4 Pass the idea on to a member of staff who is suitably incompetent and therefore guaranteed to botch it completely. Seeing one's precious idea turned into an unworkable abomination will cause a full retraction from the head, in order to avoid embarrassment and humiliation. This could lead to the

ideal situation where the head denies any knowledge of, or responsibility for, the original initiative.

5   If all else fails, try honesty! All headteachers need to be told when their suggestions are impractical or just plain daft, even if they do not like what they hear. One of my deputies was practised at calling the proverbial spade a spade and never held back on telling me what she thought. After a particular – I thought excellent – idea of mine had gone down as well as a smutty joke at a vicarage tea-party, I asked why she did not approve of it. 'Because,' she replied, 'it's complete and utter bollocks.'

I once knew of a headteacher who abruptly announced, shortly after returning from a leadership training course, that she intended to employ a zero-tolerance approach toward staff punctuality. Having decided to demonstrate her newly-found assertiveness and incisive management style, she launched herself onto the car park one morning five minutes after the bell, accosting a member of staff who had just arrived – late. Without being allowed an opportunity to explain herself, the unfortunate teacher was aggressively admonished and sent off to join her class with disapprobation ringing in her ears. It later transpired that the poor lady, having never previously been late for school during a career spanning over twenty years, had seen fit to run her elderly disabled mother to the doctors for an emergency appointment and had raced back to school in the shortest possible time. Zero-tolerance has, more recently, become all the rage, and has been applied to many aspects of school life. Zero-tolerance is what many heads publicly aspire to. Funny really, I always thought that tolerance was a virtue.

Behind every successful headteacher lies an efficient personal assistant or PA. The title is a fairly recent invention, not entirely to my liking; it seems to imply a service more similar to that provided by a valet or a maid than by a secretary, which was the accepted designation for many years. Whatever the title, the role is quite clear: to support the head at all times and in every conceivable sense, even when – and especially when – he or she is in the wrong. The archetypal head's secretary was a dragon-like creature whose prime responsibility was to guard her – invariably 'her' – boss from any manner of disturbance or interruption: a fire-breathing personification of the red traffic light. I was fortunate in never having had to endure the services of such a character and was instead extremely well-served by the four personal assistants or secretaries during my time as a head. One I worked with for only a year during a period of secondment; one retired not long after I took up my headship – I don't think I drove her away; and two were with me for many years each. All were highly competent and professional, fiercely loyal, and dedicated to the well-being of the school and its pupils and staff. They protected me from the unnecessary or the irrelevant whist alerting me to what was really important, at the same time remaining approachable and calm at all times. I could not have asked for more.

Throughout my headship I was also blessed with deputy heads and other senior colleagues who made my task so much easier and fulfilling. They too were professional and hard-working, able to keep my feet on the ground and, by means sometimes of the aforementioned strategies, successful in dissuading me from implementing some of the sillier ideas I came up with whilst driving the car or walking my dog. The senior leadership team met regularly to discuss and agree both long-term strategic vision – it is a requirement to use phrases like 'strategic vision' if you wish to get ahead in the world of education – together with shorter-term issues: crisis management some would call it. And it frequently was.

For me, the overriding headache of headship was not caused by the planned events of each day, be they meetings with staff, meetings with governors or a variety of activities which sought to constantly improve the school, all of which were usually positive and often enjoyable. It was the stuff that came at you, seemingly out of nowhere, thrown day by day to a headteacher expected to have the reserves to deal rationally with what were often the most irrational situations. I am sure many heads would agree that Harold Macmillan's response to being asked what was the biggest challenge for a statesman, could equally apply to the biggest challenge for headteachers: *'Events, my dear boy, events!'*

CHAPTER 6

The Death of the Bog-Standard Comprehensive School

'The day of the bog-standard comprehensive school is over,' announced Alastair Campbell in January 2001. Campbell, director of communications and strategy – spin doctor was the better known title – for Prime Minister Tony Blair, was a highly influential figure in the New Labour government elected in the landslide of 1997. The statement, although rapidly refuted by Education Secretary David Blunkett and later dismissed by Campbell himself as an off-the-cuff accident, came to influence education debate and policy throughout successive parliaments. The expression touched political nerves, particularly of those MPs with an ambivalence towards comprehensive schools, schools of which many of them had little or no experience. It also played on the prejudices of the popular press and the anxiety of parents, the implication being clear, that there was little future for comprehensive education in its existing format; comprehensive schools were destined for the same oblivion as the audio-cassette, Concorde and the News of the World.

The origin of the expression 'bog-standard' is unclear, there being several possibilities as to who first used it and under what circumstances. Most popular seems to be that it is a derivative of 'box standard' meaning goods displayed and sold directly from the boxed state. It may be that the words originated from the sale of children's Meccano construction sets which were available as 'box-standard' and 'box-deluxe', the former being the more basic of the two. Whereas the standard box contained a quite adequate array of parts, the deluxe was the more superior version. There has also been a suggestion, entirely without evidence it appears, that the phrase originated from the hierarchy of the BBC as a derogatory description of the values of rival independent television companies and a put-down of Lew Grade, one of ITV's most successful executives: Lew Grade being synonymous with loo-grade, ie toilet quality. The word bog, being schoolboy slang for toilet, completes the connection to bog-standard. I am however taken with the idea that the origin of bog-standard was as a late nineteenth-century acronym for 'British or German' standards of engineering, which at the time were far from ordinary, indeed of world class standard. Alas, since there is no recorded use of the expression before the 1960s, it seems that this is the least likely of all possibilities. However the expression arose, and in whatever context, its current use is to indicate something that is only mediocre, is very ordinary or less than satisfactory; the scatological connection suggests something even worse, possibly unsavoury.

Whilst examining the use of vocabulary, it is interesting to reflect how the word *satisfactory* has, in the context of education and schools, come to be devalued. Although the dictionary definition is quite clear: *'satisfactory: fit for purpose; good enough'* the word is now used to mean almost the complete opposite, ie being satisfactory is not good enough. Likewise, the word *average* has suffered similar misuse in recent times. A former secretary of state for education once publicly announced his desire to see an increase in the number of students performing above the average, demonstrating, if not ignorance of fundamental mathematics, his view that average – like satisfactory – was simply not acceptable. A very basic understanding of the concept of arithmetic mean will tell you that, if the rest of the class have gained full marks in a test or exam, an individual student's score of 99% is below average – and therefore, like my schoolboy position in the class monthly order, presumably not good enough. In a further devaluation of linguistic currency, I have read a newspaper article reporting that the purpose of the proposed introduction of starred grades for national exams was, 'to differentiate the very highest performers from the *merely* excellent' (my italics). So excellent is not so wonderful either. Merely excellent indeed! As the teacher might have told his pupil, 'Come here boy! This homework of yours was merely excellent; you will stay behind after school for detention'.

It became just a short step from bog-standard schools to failing schools. In the summer of 2003 a Sunday tabloid carried the headline: 'Death of the Local Comp' and a text which, in an outstanding piece of sensationalist journalism, described how Britain's failing comprehensive schools were to be killed off, 'consigned to the dustbin of history' and replaced by new specialist schools. A picture of a pipe-smoking Harold Wilson, castigated as the villain to blame for the creation of comprehensive schools originally, was set alongside a photograph of Charles Clarke, then Education Secretary, who was set to bring about the necessary transformation. Over the next few years the ongoing media and political trashing of the comprehensive school continued. There was renewed use of the phrase 'one-size-fits-all', in clothing terms something purchasers might be pleased to hear. In the minds of many politicians and in sections of the popular press, as far as schools were concerned, one size definitely did not, or should not, fit all. Thus, in a further denigration of the comprehensive principle, the notion became established that no single school could meet the needs of all students. There were even calls for the reintroduction of selection, something which, in most parts of the country, had disappeared back in the nineteen-seventies.

When reference is made to selective education, it is usual to couple the concept with the re-establishment of the grammar school. I seldom hear it mentioned that selection would also bring the return of the secondary modern school. These schools, it might be remembered, were attended by the majority of children, those who had failed the eleven plus. In a television debate a few years ago, a statement was made by a tabloid journalist that she had had a poor education because she had attended a comprehensive school. The association of 'poor education' with 'comprehensive school' went completely unchallenged. Comprehensive schools, it seemed, were simply not good enough for the nation's secondary school children.

I was always proud to be the head of a *comprehensive* school: a school for all children; a school which did not select its students on the basis of their ability; a school with the aim of fulfilling the different and complex needs of all learners; and a school that existed to serve its community. My school, being fully comprehensive, and therefore fully inclusive, admitted all children who had reached secondary age: students with high IQs, most of whom went on to A-level study and higher education; students with lower IQs who mostly didn't continue their education but often excelled in other ways; students who were gifted; students who were less able; students with specific learning difficulties and students with special needs. The true challenge of the comprehensive school has remained unchanged: to provide a curriculum that enables every individual to learn and achieve success at an appropriate level.

Students from my school progressed readily to further and higher education, excelled in sport and the arts, and became doctors, lawyers, scientists, teachers or entered other professions. Many settled into work locally: in retail, business or the service industry. Many now have their own children, some of whom have gone on to attend their parents' school – the wheel turned full circle. There were also students with learning difficulties, students with partial or total hearing loss, students with language disorder and students with a range of other special needs. These young people mostly all found success and fulfilment in their adult lives. There were some students with Down's syndrome. The mother of one such child told me how thrilled and proud she was to see her son in full secondary-school uniform. She was so delighted for him to move up from primary school with his peer group and, it must be said, many of his peer group and their parents had come to expect nothing less.

Of course not all comprehensive schools have excelled. In every sector, state and private, selective and non-selective, there have been underperforming schools as well as highly successful ones. Many comprehensive schools have required improvement in the quality of teaching, improvement in leadership, management and governance, and improvement in the scope and quality of the curriculum. Equally, not all schools which have failed to provide an acceptable education have been comprehensive schools; many of the sixties' grammar schools may not have stood up well to the rigour of an Ofsted inspection. Furthermore, many comprehensives that failed inspections have, with support, guidance and the dedication of their teaching staff, gone on to show substantial progress.

Successive governments have adopted a variety of means to kill off the bog-standard comprehensive school. One such tactic was the introduction of the specialist schools' programme which began with a handful of purpose-built schools in urban areas, specialising in technology. The first two of these City Technology Colleges, as they were named, opened in Nottingham and Middlesbrough in 1989. Over time the programme widened, eventually enabling all schools to apply for specialist status in one, and later two or more areas of the curriculum, the stated aim of the programme being to provide 'choice and diversity' within the secondary school sector. Schools which achieved specialist status gained additional government funding for both capital projects and running costs. There was a wide range of specialist subject areas available, the premise being that children in the latter years of primary school had developed an aptitude for one of these – science, the arts or modern languages for example. Schools were also permitted to select a proportion of their intake according to such aptitude, though in practice few ever did. It seemed to me, from the start, an extremely debatable proposition that children should select a secondary school at so young an age on the basis of subject preferences. I cannot myself recall having any such obvious or declared aptitude as a ten year-old. Assuming however the acceptance of the premise of choice and diversity, it might have been deemed sensible to offer children and their parents such choice from a variety of schools specialising in different areas of the curriculum, but this could only ever be possible if they lived in a town or city large enough to provide such variety. In a smaller conurbation or more rural situation, where pupils attended their local school (be it bog-standard or otherwise), it made little sense to me for schools to specialise in different subjects. For example, living in a particular village or small town might mean attending a school specialising in maths; living in a neighbouring locality several miles distant, with little or no public transport, could mean going to a school which specialised in sport. To attend a school of a different chosen specialism might have necessitated a return journey each day of up to thirty miles. Choice and diversity? I think not.

For these and other reasons, including the eschewing of specialism by most of my neighbouring schools, initially at least, I had felt justified in maintaining status quo. But this situation was not to last; gradually, one by one, the schools around me took the King's shilling and acquired their very own specialist status. Thinking back to my own primary-school days, I remember a playground game called sardines – a variation of bog-standard hide and seek. To begin the game a nominated person went to hide. On the count of ten, twenty or however high we could count at the time, all others set off to find the hidden one. As each person located the hide-out, they then squashed themselves into the same place alongside the others, as the proverbial sardines in a tin. There was no winner in the game, only a loser, who achieved this status by being the last to discover the whereabouts of everyone else. At the start, with perhaps a dozen playing, there was some camaraderie amongst the team, everyone rushing about together. At some later point however, and as a not too successful player of the game, I remember well the awareness, experienced suddenly, of being the only person remaining. It was a very lonely feeling, one of exclusion and failure. And so it was with the move to specialisation; just like the last sardine, there came a moment of realisation that everyone apart from me had gained specialist status, leaving my school as the one remaining bog-standard comprehensive in the area. This had not been an acceptable or comfortable place to be. Reluctantly then, but perhaps inevitably, in 2003 we set about the acquisition of specialist status.

In order to become a specialist school there were two significant hoops through which to jump: the preparation of a bid – a significant document which for us ran to some 200 pages – and the raising of a sum of £75,000 which, on successful designation, was matched by government. There followed, therefore, many months of fund-raising – I hesitate to calculate how much time, energy and indeed money were spent in raising the required amount – and countless hours writing and rewriting the bid. At one stage of the process, accompanied by one of my deputies, I took our bid – in draft form – to be scrutinised by a member of the national specialist schools' team. A trip to London – more expense – and an ascent to the umpteenth floor of a tower block on the Thames embankment, brought us face to face with a professional who was trained and experienced in assessing these bids. Like naughty school children handing in poor quality (or maybe merely excellent) work to an exasperated teacher, we sat through a devastating critique of what we had considered to be a very satisfactory effort. We had forgotten that satisfactory was not good enough. Substantial rewriting was required, we were told, if the bid was to have any chance of success and we left with a considerable challenge still ahead. It was probably as well that the building's architects had rejected the need for windows which could be opened. Such was my disillusionment that I was sorely tempted to ditch the whole application process and cast our apparently flawed paperwork into the river below.

It would be unfair however not to acknowledge that many schools have used specialism to instigate substantial improvement. But did such improvement occur as a consequence of specialising in a particular subject area? Or was it perhaps more likely the result of enhanced facilities, additional funding, increased public and media attention, and a new school name or other forms of rebranding? I was once later asked, when our bid had finally been accepted and we had shed our bog-standard status, how a visitor to my school would be able to identify our specialist subject. I replied that, hopefully, they would not. Only the logo at the foot of the printed notepaper gave this away, though when set alongside the other insignia for awards in arts, sports, healthy eating, investment in training and so on, even this did not stand out. Like many schools, the number of logos, mottos and other badges for achievement adorning our headed paper had grown to the extent that there became little room left on the page for the text of a letter.

When every, or nearly every, school had achieved specialist status, there was then a need for further advancement, in order to avoid the risk of becoming bog-standard again. So, having become a now-not-so-specialist school, we set about the acquisition of a second specialism and, later, contemplated a third. I sometimes thought that if we could have acquired specialist status in all subject areas we would have been able to call ourselves a specialist comprehensive school, though I suppose that could have defeated the whole purpose. But naturally enough it didn't stop there. Next step – most of my neighbouring schools going first again – was to become an academy. Academies are schools which are independent of so-called local authority control, funded directly from Westminster and with a number of freedoms denied to bog-standard specialist schools. And with more money.

So where will it end? When every school is a bog-standard academy will there be a need for further, additional status? How long before the new free schools, the first of which opened in 2011, also become bog-standard?

'He who rejects change is the architect of decay' – Harold Wilson again, his second appearance in this chapter. But is change always for the best? It seems to be almost an article of faith in today's world that change is synonymous with progress. How much change, particularly in education terms, is for its own sake and how much is to satisfy a short-term political agenda? It was an earlier Prime Minister, the Marquess of Salisbury I believe, who announced, probably with tongue in cheek: *'Change, change who needs change; aren't things bad enough already?'* That's one for the communication strategists and spin doctors to think about.

CHAPTER 7

A Culture of Targets

'The Ministry of Plenty's forecast had estimated the output of boots for the quarter at 145 million pairs. The actual output was given as sixty-two millions. Winston, however, in rewriting the forecast, marked the figure down to fifty-seven millions, so as to allow for the usual claim that the quota had been over-fulfilled. In any case, sixty-two millions was no nearer the truth than fifty-seven millions... Very likely no boots had been produced at all. Likelier still, nobody knew how many had been produced, much less cared.'

George Orwell 1984

Orwell's Winston Smith lived in a fictional world of the future, a world where statistics for propaganda purposes were of overwhelming and critical significance. Figures were collated and published in order to promote the ongoing success of the State. If it later transpired that the published data happened, for whatever reason, to be at odds with the truth, it was Smith's job to retract and rewrite it in such a way as to make it appear that the predictions had been accurate all along and that targets had been consistently met, if not exceeded. The data and the targets were all-important, but reflected little by way of reality.

It has become impossible to experience almost any aspect of life without encountering targets. There are targets for the Health Service, targets for Royal Mail, targets for employment, inflation and the reduction of carbon emissions. Most, if not all, government departments have targets. The police have targets for crime reduction; there are targets for recycling, for immigration and for renewable energy resources. Train and bus companies set targets for performance. Targets are fixed weekly, monthly and annually, and are used for a variety of purposes: to promote success; to produce league tables; to assess performance; and to determine bonus payments for staff.

In the National Health Service, there have been targets for waiting times to see family doctors, for hospital admission, for casualty departments and a host of other – largely non-clinical – procedures, though some were scrapped by the incoming Coalition government in the summer of 2010. There have been many reports that the achievement of targets has sometimes been put ahead of, and even at times been detrimental to, the health of patients. In 2011, a report into the failings of an NHS hospital found that the four-hour waiting time target for accident and emergency had been pursued in spite of what was always in patients' best interests. Meeting the target has become the mantra of the twenty-first century. But to what extent has all this target setting improved our experience of these services, or indeed the quality of our daily lives?

A few years ago I boarded an East Coast inter-city train bound for London at its last station before King's Cross. The train was running some twenty minutes late. After travelling just a few miles I became aware that we were slowing down; a gentle swaying of the carriage and a rattle over points indicated that we had switched from the high-speed track to the slower, suburban line. Then we stopped. The guard made an announcement apologising for the delay and informed us that we were unable to meet our target arrival time in London. So far, so good – well at least understandable. He then explained that, because of our late running, we were set to delay trains behind us, so preventing them from meeting their targets for arriving on time. It was therefore necessary for us to 'rest up' for a short while in order to allow those trains behind us to overtake. This is exactly what then happened; we all waited patiently whilst two trains sped past in order to arrive at their destination punctually. One can clearly see the logic: one train missing its target arrival time by almost three-quarters of an hour – as it turned out – was better, in management terms, than three trains missing their targets by perhaps fifteen minutes each; one train late, not three. But did this really make sense? How had the targets improved the service or the reliability? There is a moral to this particular tale: never board a train which has already missed its target time for arrival; you could be stuck all night.

There are stories – some apocryphal no doubt – of mail being 'lost' in the post because it had not been possible to meet the relevant target for delivery. A photocopier engineer, once called to repair a malfunctioning machine at my school, admitted on arrival that he knew he did not have the requisite replacement part. He was working to a specific response target. If he had made a detour to collect the necessary piece of equipment he would, he told us, have missed this target. For us the outcome was that, because of his wretched target, we had to wait whilst he returned to get the part, thus delaying the repair by significantly longer than if he'd collected it on his way. The existence of his target had resulted in a poorer service for us but, no matter, the target had been met.

There are also targets for schools of course. As a headteacher I was set targets which were agreed annually by my governing body in conjunction with a School Improvement Partner or SIP. This set-up was part of a statutory national programme – since abandoned (along with the SIPs) – for the performance management of headteachers. The targets were mostly quantitative, sometimes of dubious value, but considered necessary for the purpose of seeing how well I did my job. I always believed that spending time in school and listening to students, staff and parents would have given a much more rounded indication of my performance than relying almost exclusively on data-driven targets. My governors, I am pleased to say, being extremely practical and sensible folk, always took the more comprehensive and holistic approach to assessing my worth.

The most widely recognised target for schools is that for the percentage of its students achieving five or more good GCSE passes, where good means grades A★ to C, roughly equivalent to the old passes at O-level. These figures are published annually in league tables showing how schools are performing. In order to meet targets and show improving performance, some schools began to enter students for vocational subjects which counted for up to four passes each, only one other GCSE pass, in a second subject, being then needed to make the requisite total. Students were sometimes discouraged from taking traditional subjects such as modern languages or history as these were seen to be appreciably more difficult. In addition, some schools looked to enter their students with the examination boards which had the highest success rate. And who could blame them? Schools which were struggling, for a variety of reasons – not always all of their own making or within their control – and were possibly even under threat of closure, embarked on whatever course of action was necessary to produce an improvement in published exam performance.

Some schools, at the other end of the spectrum, often through direction of pupil choices and intensive coaching, even achieved 100% GCSE success, a remarkable outcome for schools which claimed to be genuinely comprehensive. My school had a significant number of children with special needs, some with learning difficulties that made it almost impossible for them to read or write, let alone gain five GCSEs at any grade. The pass-rate could have easily been increased had we made a decision to become less inclusive and turn away students who were never likely to be of benefit to our published statistics.

Students were not offered access to vocational courses exclusively for the purpose of boosting results. Many schools taught catering, construction and a host of other 'non-academic' subjects for all the right reasons, the prime one being that the courses were more appropriate to the needs of their students. However, in 2008 a new indicator was launched, that of five GCSE passes above grade C *including English and maths.* The addition of these subjects made the outcome very different, particularly for those schools which had relied almost exclusively on vocational courses. They saw themselves plummet down the league tables.

Fashions change – as do ministers of education who each make different demands on schools, require additional sets of data to be published and set new targets to be achieved. The last Labour government introduced the notion of floor targets for both primary and secondary schools. At secondary level, the floor target for the percentage of students gaining five or more GCSEs at grade C or higher, was set at 30%. All schools, it was decreed, should perform at or above this percentage. The target was for every school, irrespective of student intake or other factors. Many schools across the country struggled, but eventually reached this benchmark, only to find it raised to 35% in 2011 then later to 40%. It seems that the target will be lifted again at some point in the future. I can think of little more dispiriting than forever chasing a target which keeps moving away. But let's look at the floor targets in more detail. Suppose a town has 1000 students taking GCSEs, spread evenly across five schools. If each school were to achieve exactly 40% of students, that is 400, gaining the magic five good GCSEs, these schools would all have satisfied the government target. Now let's look at a second town, again with 1000 students spread across five schools, also sitting GCSEs. If the results of these schools were, say: 25%, 28%, 30%, 50%, 75% and 95%, in this town a total of just over 60% of students gained five good grades. So the first town has no failing schools; all its schools are above the floor target. But the students in the second town are achieving better: an additional 200 students have left with good grades. The government would say however that half the schools were failing!

Just as the use of targets has had an effect on the delivery of our public services, so too has the language used to describe the manner of that delivery. Train companies gave up their 'passengers' some time ago, preferring to call everyone customers. Perhaps hospital patients and school pupils might eventually also become customers? The very word 'customer' to me implies a significantly different order of relationship – that of purchaser or consumer rather than user of a service or participant in a process. The customer buys a product, be it a rail journey, an operation or an education; and of course the customer, as we know, is always right. It now seems to be the school's responsibility alone to produce exam results which show year-on-year improvement, with the student appearing to be little more than a somewhat passive recipient. Teachers now need to achieve results for their students in order to meet their own quantitative, easily-measured targets.

Surely school must be about more than just meeting targets. A young person's journey through ten or more years of compulsory education might be considered, in itself, to be as important as the eventual outcome. In my experience of travelling by train, despite my previously described complaint, arriving on time is not always all that matters. I think, for example, I would prefer to arrive a few minutes late having had the luxury of a seat, rather than having spent the entire journey standing up. Refreshments, helpful staff, panoramic views from the window all make the travelling experience more enjoyable. The journey through life itself is surely more meaningful than a simple contemplation of the final destination, given that we all know what happens to each and every one of us in the end. As Scrooge is reminded by his nephew in Dickens' well-known *Christmas Carol*, we are all 'fellow passengers to the grave'.

Recent political focus on schools' outcomes has concentrated almost exclusively on that which can be easily measured. Education reform has been centred on the delivery of qualifications to young people, on quantifying those qualifications and setting targets based solely on them. Is it any wonder that some schools have become adept at achieving results at the expense of all else? At a conference in London in the spring of 2011, I met a headteacher who described to me how he had managed to improve his school's results so that there was no longer a threat of closure. He described a timetable for his year-11 students, which took them away from many previously chosen subjects like art and drama in order to concentrate almost exclusively on maths and English. He told me that these students were denied access to extra-curricular activities, were not permitted to take part in concerts or the annual school production, and their time spent on PE and sport was severely curtailed.

And is it surprising that headteachers and schools have been driven to employ whatever legal methods – and some, sadly, illegal ones – to ensure that their targets are met? Schools have entered students for examinations equivalent to GCSEs if they are perceived to offer a greater chance of success. Pupils have been guided in their choice of subject, less by what genuinely interests them, and more by the relative ease of passing the exam. Which is more important for schools: to focus on examination performance targets or to concentrate on offering the broadest possible curriculum and the highest quality of teaching? And which will better produce well-rounded, educated citizens of the future? How much more does a good school offer than simply grinding students through an examination mill? Are our schools destined to become just exam factories?

A step back might be helpful for all of us, in order to give an opportunity for reflection on exactly what it is we want from our schools. Has the obsession with targets taken us away from the true purpose of education? Have we lost sight of the bigger picture? Do we only care about what can be measured? 1984 may have come and gone, but has it left us in a sea of statistics with data that is arguably no more valuable or reliable than that available to Winston Smith?

Albert Einstein summed it up very neatly: '*Everything that can be counted does not necessarily count; everything that counts cannot necessarily be counted.*' Politicians take note!

CHAPTER 8

Health and Safety

As a boy scout in the 1960s – scouts were all boys then – I enjoyed the whole adventure that was camping. Gilwell Park in Epping Forest, with its long scouting tradition, was one of my first camps, where we enjoyed outdoor life – under canvas but with the luxury of purpose-built showers and toilets. There were also green-field sites where the only facility was running water from an isolated tap. Hours were spent erecting tents and building bivouacs, scavenging for firewood, lighting fires and cooking on them – sausages were always a speciality: blackened and burnt beyond recognition on the outside, salmonella-raw inside.

We often travelled to camp by open lorry. Tents and all other required paraphernalia went on first, flaps at the side of the vehicle opened for ease of loading. When the gear was aboard and the sides were closed, the scouts jumped on top and the whole entourage set off. It was a sight unimaginable today – twenty or so young boys sitting atop a mound of camping equipment – no seat belts and little protection from other traffic. As we left the town we sped along main roads and country lanes with wind in our woggles, oblivious to any concept of potential danger.

My scout uniform was enhanced by the wearing of a sheath-knife attached to my belt. These knives were sold widely in high-street shops, had blades of six inches or so, and sat in leather holsters which were often home-made. I still have the sheath which was home to the knives I had owned during my scouting years, though the weapons themselves are long gone. We used the knives for a variety of purposes – all then legal – from food preparation to the whittling of sticks; with moderate skill and much patience we would fashion excellent whistles from small branches of elder. The knives were also used for playing a game called splits which involved throwing your knife close to, but not at, your opponent. At camp we cut and chopped wood with bow-saws and axes. Proficient use of the axe contributed towards a badge which accredited skill as a craftsman rather than – if there were such an award today – as a mass murderer. I'm sure there must have been accidents but the risks were presumably deemed acceptable; I recall no visits to hospital casualty as a result of mortal wound or stabbing.

Scout Bob-a-Job Week, renamed simply Job Week when a shilling – or bob – no longer seemed suitable reward for any task well done, was axed in 1999 as a result of concerns over safety. The movement's founder, Baden-Powell, had first introduced a good turn day in 1914; Bob-a-Job Week started officially in 1949. For fifty years, cubs and scouts would, during the school Easter holiday, travel from door-to-door offering to undertake tasks or run errands in exchange for a shilling – or five pence – towards scouting funds. Cutting lawns, sweeping paths, chopping logs(!) and cleaning cars were all part of the repertoire. Some scouts encountered more unusual activities: washing elephants at a zoo was probably the most bizarre recorded. But all fell foul of health and safety culture when particular fears for potential child abuse were acknowledged and it was thought that, for their own welfare, young people should not be allowed to knock on the doors of strangers. The Scout movement has since adopted other means of fundraising. In an attempt at some kind of revival of Job Week, a new approach to undertaking good works has been actively considered, involving scouts working as a group and accompanied by a leader. In other words, with all the fun taken out.

Scouting was not the only activity of my younger days that entailed elements of risk which are no longer accepted. After taking A-levels, I hitchhiked across the Continent with a friend. The era of cheap flights had not yet arrived and the railways were prohibitively expensive. The only practical way to see Europe on a student budget was by thumbing lifts. Hitchhikers were a common sight in this country and abroad, many motorists being willing to offer lifts without fear for the safety of either themselves or their non-paying passengers. That the practice has virtually disappeared may be because of more affordable transport options or, perhaps more likely, because motorists have become conscious of the potential for danger either from or to the hitchhikers. Undoubtedly drivers who take strangers in their cars are now very aware that they put themselves at potential risk of accusation of abuse, a situation most are unwilling to countenance. In 1970 however, such fears were not prevalent; I travelled with a friend across Belgium and France, through Germany and Switzerland and returned safely, at little to no cost. We were shown great acts of kindness: meals and drinks were offered and, on one occasion – in a town in the south of Germany – we were given a bed for the night by a couple who, as they were preparing to drop us off from a lift, realised that we were too late to find any alternative accommodation.

Just as increased awareness of personal wellbeing has affected the practice of hitchhiking, so too have other aspects of road use been significantly influenced by safety concerns. Although legislation has required the fitting of front seat belts in new cars since 1963, the wearing of them was not made compulsory until twenty years later. Cars built earlier, though still thoroughly roadworthy, were exempt. My first proudly-owned vehicle, a Ford Anglia with a custom painted roof and magnificently underpowered engine, did not have the luxury of seat belts. My second car, also a Ford, was fitted with belts and we *did* wear them. This was most apposite given that I turned the car over with three friends inside, returning at speed from the Isle of Wight festival where we had just seen Jimi Hendrix appear in his last ever concert.

It is reliably estimated that the seat belt has saved hundreds of lives every year. 'Clunk Click – every trip,' was the imperative slogan for the irritating but influential television commercials of the nineteen-seventies. I certainly was a fortunate beneficiary of the seat belt legislation, as too were my friends. And the law, very sensibly, went further. Crash helmets for motor cyclists were made compulsory in 1973; prior to that riders of motorbikes and scooters mostly drove bare-headed. My first and only ride as pillion on a Lambretta was without any kind of head protection and now seems to have been unnecessarily dangerous and foolhardy.

Accepting that legislation has helped improve the safety of road users, the law has more recently taken to concerning itself with other facets of the Nation's health and welfare. Legislation on smoking has changed radically since the time when it was seen to be 'cool' to light up a cigarette. Smoking in cinemas was commonplace in my student days, though eventually restricted to one side of the auditorium – the right facing the screen if I remember correctly. Passengers who wished to smoke on London Transport buses were required to sit upstairs. No smoking carriages on trains and the tube gradually became the rule rather than the exception, until smoking was banned completely on the underground network following the King's Cross fire in 1987. Twenty years later, smoking was banned in all indoor public places, including bars and restaurants. Smoking in cars may well be next. In a few years from now it will undoubtedly seem quite incredible that there was ever a time when smoking indoors was allowed.

I suppose the issue with 'Health and Safety' – a now often mimicked and derided expression – is one of balance and common sense. The 'elf-an-safety-gone-mad' brigade has had a field day with stories of seemingly senseless application of rules: the pantomime performers banned from throwing sweets from the stage to children in the audience in case someone got hurt; outlawing the playing of conkers or throwing of snowballs in the school playground – indeed playground games at all in some cases. We have Christmas crackers which cannot be purchased by under-sixteens because they contain 'explosives', hanging baskets and overhead decorations which have been removed in case they fall and hit passers-by, and sun-lotion which must be sprayed onto the faces and limbs of school children without the need for rubbing in and thereby making physical contact. Have things not all gone way over the top? As the Prime Minister, David Cameron said at the Conservative Party conference in 2011, 'Britannia didn't rule the waves with her arm-bands on.'

In school, health and safety is a constant concern. Nothing is more important to any headteacher than the welfare of students in his or her care. 'In loco parentis' was the phrase used to describe the role of school teachers and it remains a sensible one. It is surely self-evident that one would supervise and care for other people's children at least as well as one would one's own. The difference is – I suggest – that most parenting and supervision of our own children is built around old-fashioned common sense, rather than through obedience to the law or to edicts of policy.

Much of the concern over health and safety is relevant, but there are areas where it has severely restricted school activity. For example, some schools have curtailed or completely ceased the practice of taking students on trips away from home. I am pleased to say that, thanks to the commitment of my staff, we were able to maintain a programme of residential and adventurous activities, though when students were safely returned home from such ventures, I must admit to always experiencing a deep sense of relief. Canals, rivers and mountains were all potential sources of danger; abseiling and climbing, canoeing and sailing, cycling on and off road – all hazardous. Even after the most careful planning and extensive risk-assessment, taking young people away on outdoor pursuits inevitably means increased opportunity for accident. Although I understood the reasons why some headteachers considered the risks too great, I always felt it to be a great pity that they abandoned many of their more adventurous trips and visits.

The most cumbersome part of a school's duty to keep its pupils safe is probably the need for Criminal Records Bureau or CRB checks. The CRB was established in 2002 following an acceptance by British police forces that they did not have sufficient resources to process the huge number of record checks being requested. The service offered by the CRB enables schools and other organisations, in both the public and private sectors, to ensure that unsuitable applicants for work involving children or vulnerable adults are identified. The checks are also available to voluntary organisations, to similarly protect themselves from individuals who may have a record of convictions and cautions.

But there is a degree of nonsense about. The checks appear not to separate important and relevant criminal history from that which is trivial. A mature applicant for an administrative post at my school had a caution as a young teenager for stealing a packet of sweets unearthed following a CRB check. I have also come across situations where an individual has been investigated by police following a false allegation but, on finding no grounds for further action, the incident has none the less been recorded on file. Given that anyone, at any time, is potentially at risk of accusation, however spurious, this is a worrying trend. Guilty even if unfounded or unproven appears to be the modus operandi here.

The need to be checked for potential past criminal activity has undoubtedly dissuaded otherwise willing volunteers from becoming involved in youth clubs and other work with young people. The premise seems to be that such volunteers need to prove their innocence and some have, quite reasonably, declined to do so. Perhaps a past minor shoplifting offence – or a 25 pence fine for a student rag week stunt – might deter some folks from putting themselves forward. Then there is the question of who is to be checked. If you take children on a residential trip, staying in a hotel, an accompanying adult would need to be checked. But what about the other guests in the hotel? How about the staff: chambermaids and waiters? When students on a day trip to Boulogne or a half-term ski trip cross the Channel by ferry, should schools insist on all passengers and crew being CRB checked? Adults come in contact with children continually. My paperboy frequently engages with grown-ups on his morning round; not all his customers are, like me, police-checked. To make matters worse, the checks are not portable from one working or volunteering situation to another. Despite teachers being fully cleared for their existing posts, if they move schools or offer to assist with a local youth activity on a regular basis, they have to start all over again. People who have moved jobs frequently, or have several part-time posts and taken on a range of voluntary activities involving young people have drawers full of CRB certificates.

Some of the saddest repercussions of our health and safety culture are those where life has been put at risk or even lost because of a strict adherence to the rule book. There have been occasions where police and fire crews were unable, in certain situations, to effect a rescue because of a potential breach of health and safety regulations. It is also sadly the case that members of the public have become increasingly reluctant or unwilling to come to the aid of distressed or injured individuals for fear of allegation of wrong-doing. In the extreme, a motorist may be thought unwise to attend to a distressed young person stranded by the roadside, for fear of potential accusation of abuse.

The influence of the State moved closer to home when the food and drink we consume on a daily basis came under the microscope. We all understand the importance of healthy eating; 'You are what you eat' was the slogan of a few years back. But the regulations imposed on schools with regard to what could be provided for students to eat in their break and lunchtimes became over-prescriptive and unworkable. Healthy eating in schools is a world where the school kitchen is preparing Jamie Oliver-style bean and lentil pasta whist parents are pushing beefburgers and chips to their hungry kids through the school railings. Obesity is now a well-recognised problem affecting a large proportion of the population, and it is surely appropriate for schools to be closely involved in educating children about options for healthy eating. But again, legislation has eclipsed common sense and done little, I believe, to make a lasting impression on the eating habits of the nation's young people. For a time, some of my students enjoyed school lunches prepared and cooked by themselves, working alongside members of staff. A healthy home-cooked meal, partly the students' own work, was served on a daily basis. Unfortunately 'health and safety' intervened and, because of food preparation regulations – some sensible, but others unnecessarily bureaucratic – the service was forced to close.

Healthy eating has not crossed the traditional boundaries of all school kitchens, nor been fully embraced by everyone. A school cook I encountered during a period of secondment, whose idea of healthy eating was to put a lettuce leaf in the hot-dogs or a slice of tomato in the bacon rolls (both garnishes being readily discarded in the nearest waste bin), employed an unusual method of purchasing and storing bread for sandwiches. She would buy a complete week's worth of sliced bread on a Sunday and store it all in the fridge until the last was used on a Friday. Thus it became a rule amongst staff never to buy a sandwich after Wednesday at the latest. Even then, because of a wish to keep costs to a minimum, she would use the crusts of the loaf in the sandwich, positioning them to face inwards in their triangular plastic containers so that the rogue slices could not be detected until after the purchase had been made. On the occasion of a visit from inspectors, she produced for us a very acceptable lunch served in my office. The sandwiches were fine – it was only Tuesday – and there was a range of other well-presented edible treats, but as a finishing touch she had prepared a large plateful of turkey twizzlers, a delicacy which had come to represent the nadir of school cuisine. Turkey twizzlers had been repeatedly pronounced by government food tsars to be more dangerous to the health of young people than passive – or possibly even active – smoking. I had wrongly assumed them to have long since been struck off the menu. In an effort to hide these universally-reviled beasts from the inspectors and prevent an inadequate judgement on healthy eating, I managed to whisk them off the serving trolley when attention was diverted and hide them under my desk. Only later did I discover that, although out of my line of sight, they had remained clearly visible to the inspectors from where they had been sitting, wondering no doubt why I kept a platter of skewered meat on the floor by my feet.

By the time I retired, machines in schools selling fizzy drinks and sweets had become as extinct as the dinosaur. As for potato crisps, they were held to be so sinful that some primary schools attempted to forbid children from bringing them in their lunch-boxes. A newspaper cartoon of the time depicted a picture of a naughty schoolboy caught smoking by one of his teachers. 'I'm only smoking,' the student was saying, 'to hide the smell of crisps on my breath!'

CHAPTER 9

The Craft of the Classroom

Some headteachers teach. They say that the classroom is their refuge from the stresses and strains of running a school and that teaching children is, after all, why they originally came into the profession. Others regard classroom teaching as an indulgence which takes them away from more important matters. They employ teaching staff to do the actual teaching. Some, one suspects, have become so rusty or tarnished that they would simply no longer be able to survive in the classroom.

My own teaching load varied throughout my headship years and often changed mid-term. Sometimes I was without a regular timetable, my contact with students in the classroom limited to covering for absent colleagues. This was always a good way to keep a watchful eye on what others had been teaching – snooping one might say. When I did have a regular teaching commitment I took classes for science – physics greatly preferred; my chemistry knowledge was weak and my biology virtually non-existent, confined largely to a first-year grammar-school study of the amoeba.

I also became a part-time member of the mathematics department. When I first suggested that the most able students in maths should take an accelerated course of study, sit GCSE a year early, then begin A-level study in year 11, the head of the maths department agreed wholeheartedly with the idea – so long as it would be me who taught them. Reluctant at first, but not for long – headteachers can be very egocentric – I decided to take on the project. It turned out to be an immense pleasure, teaching one of the most responsive groups of students I have ever encountered. We raced through the syllabus: trigonometry and algebra; simultaneous and quadratic equations; Euclid and Pythagoras; probability curves and normal distributions. This was a class of highly motivated students, eager and keen to learn; and they all gained top grades at GCSE.

As the years progressed and classroom technology raced ahead, I began to feel more and more out of touch with the day-to-day process of classroom teaching – deskilled even. The interactive whiteboard was my nemesis. Being brought up with blackboard and chalk – I still possessed my set of white and coloured chalks in their very own Golden Virginia tobacco tin – I had learned my art with board ruler, protractor and the giant-sized compasses that resembled some kind of weapon of torture. The ordinary write-on whiteboard was something of a welcome improvement: no longer were one's clothes covered in chalk dust – though hands and sleeves were instead stained with board ink. The interactive board however, was computer technology beyond the space-age: an electronic pen which created diagrams and graphs at will; shapes that could be moved and rotated with a tap on the screen; previous work brought back to view without so much as the click of a mouse. No more the frustration caused by another teacher unwittingly wiping the blackboard of work which had been painstakingly prepared and purposely left for future use with other classes. A very experienced maths teacher told me, when one of these monsters had been installed in her classroom, that she would never get the hang of operating the thing and that it was about as much use as a hot-air balloon on the Moon. After a couple of sessions training and a few weeks of practice, she became so adept, competent and attached to the new device that, on suffering a power cut one day, she felt almost unable to teach her classes.

But new gadgetry has not been the only significant change for teachers in the last three decades. Contracts of employment and workload have also seen major reform. At one time activities such as attendance at parents' evenings, writing reports and involvement in after-school meetings were considered to be voluntarily undertaken and not formally part of teachers' duties. During the 1970s, teacher unions used this as a lever in the not-so-delicate process of pay bargaining. At times of high inflation, the securing of annual salary increases became an integral part of the education calendar. A union submission of a 20% pay claim would typically be met by an employers' offer of 10%. After weeks of dispute and unrest, leading to eventual arbitration, the final settlement would be an honest compromise of 15%. The unrest would usually take the form of what was grandly called 'withdrawal of goodwill'. Whilst this might sound like a failure to hold doors open for others or relinquishing one's seat on a bus for an elderly or infirm individual, it was, in fact, a refusal to undertake these so-called voluntary duties. The Education Reform Act of 1988, in addition to much other legislation, redefined teachers' employment to make these activities a formal part of their contracts; no longer could teachers take action like withdrawal of goodwill without loss of pay. It was strike or nothing. The act also made compulsory the attendance, not just at after-school meetings, but for five days annually – taken from school holidays – for the purpose of staff training. These days, subsequently named Baker days, after the architect of the new legislation, quickly became an established part of the school year and an essential component of schools' development.

More change was to come. In 2003, a workload agreement swept away many administrative tasks previously undertaken routinely by qualified teachers, in order to free up staff for their prime responsibility of teaching. These duties – chores some might have argued – included the collecting of children's dinner-money; preparing and setting up classroom displays; ordering equipment; and monitoring data. But perhaps the two most significant changes came a little later. Exam invigilation had been, for most of my teaching career, an accepted part of every summer term. When year 11 students were sitting their GCSE and other examinations, teaching staff, freed from part of their classroom commitment, would routinely perform the duty of supervision. Pacing up and down between rows of desks; handing out supplementary sheets of paper to the enslaved candidates; watching the clock hardly move: this was the business of exam invigilation. I was told of a game played in the examination hall by staff, intent on some relief from boredom, called invigilation tag. Moving silently and surreptitiously between the ranks of exam desks so as to avoid any disturbance to the candidates, the teacher who was 'on' would slowly criss-cross the room until he (not she – only men would indulge themselves in such immaturity) could tag another invigilator who then became 'on'. The beauty of the game, apparently – I was never personally drawn to this kind of juvenile indulgence – was that it could be played in the presence of up to maybe 200 students, none of whom would be remotely aware of what was going on around them.

Away from the examination hall, there were other games that could be played. 'Smuggling clichés', a game for two or more players, was a kind of Radio Four-type panel game, a cross between *I'm Sorry I Haven't a Clue* and *The Unbelievable Truth*. During the course of a poorly chaired meeting – one with an interminably long agenda where discussion was allowed to drag on remorselessly – in order to relieve the tedium or just to lighten the mood, the players had to drop in stereotypical phrases or clichés without the other players being aware. Thus one could attempt to sneak in the words 'when all is said and done', declare a wish not to 'reinvent the wheel' or employ the monstrously over-used expression 'at the end of the day'. A pre-arranged signal would be given by one or more of the other contestants if the phrase was spotted. Or one could try the introduction of a mixed metaphor. A deputy headteacher I once worked with was the master, or rather mistress, of this grammatical gyration. I heard her announce to a full staff meeting – on one of the few occasions in the late seventies when goodwill was prevalent – that if we failed to comply with the latest regulations from on high, we would be 'batting on thin ice'. On another occasion, the leaving of a decision to fate would be 'all in the lap of chance'. A colleague of mine, in a later meeting at which the dear lady was present, managed to smuggle through a phrase warning us all of the danger of 'skating on a sticky wicket.' She did not notice.

Probably the biggest relief of all for teachers, however, was the removal in 2008 of the requirement to routinely cover classes for colleagues who were absent from school. Staff cover was an onerous and sometimes difficult task, especially when teachers encountered students they did not usually teach and who were perhaps unknown to them. For young or inexperienced colleagues, a cover lesson was enough to cast an unwelcome shadow over the whole day. And sometimes, especially in the winter or during times of high absence through illness, one could be asked, or indeed possibly instructed, to take a cover lesson two or three times a week. For some this represented a loss of all non-contact time.

When the workload agreement was introduced, the burden of cover reduced substantially. Save in the event of an emergency, cover came to be undertaken by separately-engaged supply teachers or other, non-qualified staff known as cover supervisors. The role of the cover supervisors was not to teach the classes but to give students work which had been previously set by other teachers. Supply staff were brought into school for planned teacher absence or, at the last minute, to take the lessons of colleagues who were ill. During a period when I was acting deputy head, I once escorted a gentleman, who had arrived at reception after the start of the first lesson, straight up to the classroom, without much by way of explanation. I left him to his fate and returned to my office. A few minutes later, I received a call from reception informing me that the awaited supply teacher had just arrived. So who had I taken to the classroom? In the end the misunderstanding was easily resolved. The prospective candidate for a teaching post on an informal visit to the school had been too polite to object, imagining that he had been deliberately thrown in at the deep end in order to test his resilience and strength of character.

For newly-qualified teachers, the first year's teaching is a steep learning curve. I was brought up on Michael Marland's widely-acknowledged survival guide: *The Craft of the Classroom*, which was packed with practical help for new teachers on everything from the taking of registers to the collecting in of homework. There was also, for the start of the academic year in September, the mantra 'not to smile before Christmas' – a warning to newcomers in the profession of the danger of early familiarity with one's charges.

It is hard to believe now that, up until as late as the 1970s, it was not necessary for a university graduate to undertake any form of training in order to teach; a degree was the only licence required to enter the classroom. This may go some way to explaining why schools in the sixties were staffed by many well-meaning but often ineffectual graduates, fluent in their subject but unable to command respect or induce any significant degree of learning. It also accounted for much of my own grammar-school experience. The situation today is much improved. With well-established post-graduate training and comprehensive induction for newly-qualified teachers, no longer are raw recruits unleashed on classes of up to thirty adolescents and left to sink or swim. If post-graduate teaching practice is akin to driving with L-plates, the first year of teaching is equivalent to having a set of P-plates which denote a recent driving test pass. There are undoubtedly still some teachers who struggle in the classroom, but in my opinion the profession has never been so well trained and qualified.

As a result of the contractual reforms, teaching has become a much more professional activity. Freed from administrative tasks, exam invigilation and staff cover, teachers have more time for the planning and preparation of lessons. But they have had to become far more accountable. I have encountered several hundred teachers during my career and, as a head, appointed scores. Apart from a very few who found teaching difficult – those who couldn't rather than wouldn't – and a few on the lazy side – those who wouldn't rather than couldn't – the teachers I have known and worked with have all been conscientious professionals. Usually, when a teacher is working below an acceptable standard, improvement can be achieved through discussion, support and regular monitoring. When this approach is not successful, more formal proceedings can follow. I have sat through hearings of both competence and conduct but, in proportion to the total number of teachers employed at my school, thankfully few. Sometimes newly-qualified teachers find, in the first year of full-time teaching, that the job is not for them; some have struggled to enforce reasonable discipline and others simply found the workload too heavy.

In past years, before I became a head, I witnessed some teachers, especially senior teachers, who managed to use administrative tasks as an excuse to hide from the classroom. Deputy heads who spent their days organising school stationery – a prerequisite for promotion to senior management as we have seen – showing visitors around the school, arranging flowers or setting out chairs for assembly, were by no means uncommon. Furniture was so much better behaved than children and did not answer back or produce work for marking. And the pay was better. By the time I retired from my headship, the role of the teacher had become firmly established as being solely responsible for teaching and learning. Senior staff were responsible for the same, especially the monitoring of standards and the professional development of teachers who had been set free from the myriad other tasks traditionally associated with the role.

So the real craft of the classroom is not about pacing the examination room, collecting dinner-money or covering for absent colleagues. Ordering exercise books and counting paper clips are no longer part of the job. One of the genuinely positive changes to bring about direct improvement for the education of school pupils has been to allow teachers to do what they do best – teach!

CHAPTER 10

An Inspector Calls

It is hard to imagine life as a headteacher without Ofsted, the Office for Standards in Education. Created in 1992, this national scheme of school and college inspection replaced a local authority-based one conducted by HMI – Her Majesty's Inspectorate. HMI inspections were more infrequent than those that came after, but were no less thorough. In my 18 years in schools prior to 1992, I encountered only one official school inspection; in the same period after, I was 'fortunate' to experience almost a dozen.

The most significant difference between the two regimes is that, whereas HMI inspection reports were shared with the school, the local authority and the Secretary of State, they remained unpublished. Ofsted reports, as any schoolchild will tell you, are available for all to see: inspection reports appear on the Ofsted website. It is also a requirement that parents are provided with copies, and students are given a summary of the report in a short – sometimes rather condescending – letter from the lead inspector. And local newspapers are never slow to print stories, based on inspection reports, of the successes – or failures – of their neighbourhood schools.

My first Ofsted experience whilst a headteacher was in1996

when a team of twenty, comprising HMI and the newly-trained registered inspectors, descended. We had been given a ludicrous period of notice – several months. This was one of the aspects which eventually changed, with the notice being reduced to two days or even less. Sometimes it happened that inspectors arrived at a school without prior warning and completely unannounced. I had sometimes wondered whether, perhaps as an April fool's joke, I might turn up at another school and announce to the receptionist that I was an Ofsted inspector arriving to conduct a no-notice inspection. The hoax would be quickly discovered, but not before many pulses had been set racing. It now appears that, following the appointment of a new head of the inspection service in January 2012, no-notice inspections may be set to become the norm.

The first national round of inspections involved an almost unbelievable collection of paperwork which was required by inspectors in advance. In the week prior to my first Ofsted experience, the lead inspector collected over a dozen boxes of school policies, records, minutes of meetings and subject schemes of work. It had taken weeks to amass the required documentation, some of which – it must be admitted – had been especially written for the occasion. In common with other schools undergoing the same ordeal, hours had been spent drafting and redrafting page after page of policy in the sure and certain knowledge that, after the inspection was over, most of it would be unlikely ever to be read again. File upon file, box upon box, the documentation was gathered in my office, covering enough floor space to constitute its very own health and safety hazard. It was necessary, when the time came for all this to be collected, for a forklift truck-style operation to load the contents into the inspector's awaiting delivery van.

Before the inspection, all parents had received a questionnaire to be returned – in a sealed envelope if so desired – with responses to around twenty questions asking opinions of their child's school. One parent returned his with a wax seal on the envelope, presumably to prevent me peeking or tampering with the contents. Given the history of this individual's unrealistic expectations of the school and his willingness to complain endlessly about everything, it was extremely tempting to open the envelope, if not to accidentally lose it down the back of a filing cabinet. In addition to the questionnaire responses – as if these were not enough – there was also a pre-inspection meeting for parents. Originally it had been prescribed that teachers who happened to have their own children attending the school would be barred from such meetings; certainly those who didn't were allowed nowhere near. I suppose the hypothesis was that a draconian headteacher or other overpowering member of staff, if present, would prevent parents from speaking out. 'There must be something wrong with this school, maybe quite a lot, which I want you to tell me about,' the nice inspector man or woman might have said; or perhaps they didn't. I wouldn't have known: I wasn't allowed to be there. It certainly all gave the impression that inspectors thought the school had something to hide and that parents, without teachers present, would be able to convey otherwise hidden opinions. In the end it turned out that there were few complaints; those that did surface were mainly about homework. Some parents thought there was not enough homework set; others that there was too much. There's just no pleasing people. The questionnaires, when we were allowed to see them – or rather a summary of them – indicated that the overwhelming majority of parents were more than happy with their children's education.

In 2005, the concept of school self-evaluation was introduced, with schools compiling a self-evaluation form or SEF (everything in education has an acronym) to be made available to inspectors. Schools therefore evaluated themselves. Ofsted evaluated the school's own evaluation; sometimes HMI were present, to evaluate Ofsted's evaluation of the school's evaluation. At the very top, ministers evaluated HMI's evaluation of Ofsted's evaluation of the school's evaluation. Nobody escaped evaluation, except the ministers, but then they had their electorate to answer to. When, in 2010, the Coalition government told Ofsted to ditch the SEF, it was for the stated reason of removing the bureaucratic burden of form-filling and allowing heads to get on with their jobs. You could almost hear the cheers from schools across the land.

An essential part of any inspection process is the observation of classroom lessons. Being observed has become a commonplace occurrence in any teacher's routine, though it might be pertinent to ask whether what is seen by an outsider is always a true reflection of normal practice. An essential understanding of research into social behaviour requires the need to be extremely wary of the effect of outside observation on the behaviour being studied. It is not dissimilar from looking at the behaviour of fundamental particles, where in order to see what is going on, one must at least shine light or other radiation. The particles being observed however are so infinitesimally small that their motion is affected by the very shining of the light. So what you see is not what would be happening were you not to be looking. Is it like this in the classroom? Does the presence of an inspector or other observer affect students' behaviour and work ethic? A teacher I once knew told his class of students, who were not always particularly well behaved, that the inspector likely to be coming in to observe the lesson was in fact the headteacher of a newly-opened, special boarding unit looking to recruit naughty children. Needless to say, when the inspector arrived, the students conducted themselves impeccably and the teacher was praised for his excellent classroom management and control.

Inspectors, whilst observing a lesson, will tour the classroom looking at the work of individual students and asking questions to ascertain the level of understanding and to check whether suitable progress is being made. In one of my own lessons – always scary: what if the head were found to be an inadequate teacher? – the inspector asked a boy to tell him about what he was working on and was summarily told to mind his own business, though in language considerably less polite. On another occasion, in a maths lesson, the inspector sat next to a girl who had been obstreperous and unco-operative since the beginning of the year. Although she was well-behaved on this occasion, she had a history of being distracted, talking overmuch and seldom listening fully when I was teaching. 'Oh I hate maths,' I heard her say to the sharp-suited man from the ministry who appeared to be writing down her comments verbatim. 'I can't understand any of it and he never explains a thing.' How about that for rough justice I thought – I expect her mother had echoed the sentiments in the returned questionnaire. Fortunately, other students were less critical of my classroom performance; they proceeded to offer the inspector a more accurate picture of my teaching – to my mind – and allowed me to retain some degree of confidence and integrity.

As the years passed, one full inspection followed another – roughly one every three years – with other visits and progress checks in between, each encounter bringing its own particular blend of stress and pressure. The initial phone call informing me of an upcoming inspection set off the nerves every time and always created that uncomfortable feeling of butterflies in the stomach – though for me they usually felt more like locusts. And an immediate sense of panic, even knowing that the school was in good shape and there was no real need to worry. It was always, 'What if something goes uncommonly wrong during the inspection?' The press has highlighted certain practices allegedly employed by some schools to improve their chances of a successful inspection outcome. It has been claimed that these schools sought to remove their most troublesome students for the period of inspection by means of exclusion – formal or otherwise – sending them out on a school visit or even persuading them to truant. It has also been alleged that some schools coerced certain teachers into going off sick, so that they would not be observed teaching. These tales of schools 'cheating' may well be exaggerated; certainly one might tweak things a little but HMI and registered inspectors are no fools and any obvious subterfuge would be readily found out, one would hope. The inspectors are also human – well most of them, most of the time – and with the odd exception are genuinely committed to fair play, honesty and sometimes a degree of discretion.

In twenty years of the Ofsted regime, there have been considerable changes in frequency, length and focus of inspections: from teams of twenty in school for a week, to one or two inspectors for just a couple of days; from several months advance notice, to a phone call the day before; from lorry loads of paperwork, to a few sides of A4. Between 2006 and 2010 there was an additional duty on schools to provide evidence of much wider aspects of children's education and well-being. Under the universal phrase *Every child matters* came the necessity to demonstrate that children kept fit through sport and exercise, ate healthily, were prepared economically for working life, and contributed to the promotion of community cohesion (whatever that meant).

Despite my nervousness and apprehension, the outcome of each of my inspections was very positive. Although we never reached the highest category of *outstanding* we usually came out as *good* with particular features which were *outstanding*. On only one occasion was the verdict a bitter disappointment, but that is a story for another chapter. It does seem though, that schools and colleges are often made to jump through the hoops only to find the bar raised – I can do mixed metaphors too – and what was once an acceptable level of education is no longer. The current chief of Ofsted announced, before taking up his appointment, that there were too many outstanding schools. What could he have meant? Given that *outstanding* was a closely defined criterion, was the implication that inspectors had got their judgements wrong. Or did he simply mean that outstanding did not mean what it said?

Of course we must all, as professionals, be accountable; we must all strive to provide the very best education and care for our students; and we must all be open to positive criticism and improvement where necessary. The question is whether this is best enhanced or supported by the existing regime of inspection. J B Priestley's inspector called unannounced – like his Ofsted namesake seemingly could in future – and wreaked havoc among an erstwhile happy family, causing upset and turmoil, and leading them to question their attitudes and values. He left his visitors promising 'fire and blood and anguish' if lessons were not learned. Some headteachers might feel similarly threatened by the inspector from Ofsted.

CHAPTER 11

The Curriculum Pendulum

Since 1989, when I became a headteacher, the Department for Education and Science or DES, as it was then known, has been renamed and rebranded no fewer than five times under as many prime ministers and more than twice as many different education secretaries. Each incoming secretary of state, however he or she names or styles their department, being eager to prove themselves worthy of the title, has sought new solutions to the perceived woes of the British education system. Thus, from John MacGregor, who lasted little over a year, to Michael Gove, who at the time of writing is currently in post, we have seen change upon change – one new initiative upon another – and funding for specifically targeted projects allocated, only to be later withdrawn in order to provide cash for the next idea. Usually the reforms are introduced with good intention though, I fear, often for party political advantage and without significant lasting success.

That is not to suggest that change and improvement were never needed. There have been several positive developments and much progress made, but many reforms of school structure and curriculum have not been given sufficient time to become established before a change of minister or government has swept them away in order to promote new priorities. With the lifetime of a parliament being around four years, and that of the minister in charge only two years on average, the issue is not just one of political interference but equally – with continual eye to the next election and, dare I suggest, on the career prospects of the minister – of the constant need for a short-term boost in the poll ratings.

In October 2011, on the eve of the Conservative Party conference, the Secretary of State for Education announced that the teaching of a modern foreign language in schools would be made compulsory for all children from the age of five. His reasoning seemed sound, and I found myself unable to disagree with his proposition. However, five-year olds in September 2012, the suggested starting date of the programme, would not be leaving school until at least 2023 – possibly later, depending on the progress of legislation to raise the school-leaving age. Assuming that the modern language would be taught throughout the individual's time at school, the first cohort to benefit fully would – on past averages – span three parliaments and up to six secretaries of state. Few past initiatives have lasted anywhere near that length of time.

The requirement for schools to teach modern languages is nothing new; the introduction of the National Curriculum made the study of a foreign language by all secondary pupils compulsory. This requirement was partially axed in 2004, when fifteen and sixteen year-olds were exempted and languages became optional again for students in this age range. In 2010, the re-introduction of a modern language up to school-leaving age was effectively made compulsory once more with the introduction of the English Baccalaureate, of which more later. Returning to the primary school curriculum, a proposal to introduce a compulsory foreign language for five year-olds was first advanced in 2002. Time and money were invested in long term preparation for an eventual implementation. However, in 2010, one of the first acts of the Coalition government was to shelve the new proposals, whereupon many local authorities shed their primary language advisors and we witnessed the unravelling of much detailed preparation and planning. This groundwork would surely need to be re-commissioned if languages were to be made compulsory again. This is all a classic example of the continual vacillation which I have termed 'the curriculum pendulum'.

There have been many other examples of the curriculum pendulum in action. In secondary schools, technology became a compulsory subject for all students, again as the result of the introduction of the National Curriculum, only for the compulsion to be later rescinded. In recent years schools have seen the literacy hour, citizenship, catch-up programmes and one-to-one tuition come and go. Whatever happened to *Every Child Matters* – the political brain-child of the last years of the Labour government? This portfolio included aspects of child health, safety and welfare, in addition to the requirement for young people to enjoy and achieve, though I always suspected that politicians viewed the achievement factor as more important than the enjoyment one. All this was ditched without ceremony by the incoming government of 2010; it would appear that every child only mattered for the space of a few years. There have been initiatives for students labelled 'gifted and talented' – popularly known as G and T, though without the ice and slice – promoted and funded, then later quietly abandoned. Coursework for GCSE has come and gone. Modular exams look set for the chop, Michael Gove having directed that from 2012 all subjects at GCSE should be tested by terminal examinations only. The curriculum pendulum fully in action!

Another example of politically unhelpful about-turns is that of the Schools' Sports Partnership. This initiative – launched in 2003 – involved the establishment of, and funding for, partnerships between secondary and primary schools, with a specific remit to increase sporting opportunities for children. The build up to the London Olympics was seen to be an additional opportunity to promote sport for all. However, an announcement to scrap the partnerships was made in 2010, only for there to be a partial U-turn some months later.

Now here's a revolutionary thought: perhaps there could be some degree of cross-party support and full agreement with headteachers and schools to introduce – and fund – a project such as modern languages for all children from the age of eight, guaranteed to be maintained – without substantial change – for fifteen years. If learning a modern language is such a good idea in 2012, why might it be any less so in 2027? Why should the teaching of French, German or Spanish be any kind of party political issue? Come to that, why should any school curriculum decision be a matter exclusively for politicians?

Fortunately there have been some constants. Despite much revision, the GCSE, which replaced the old CSE and O-level exams, has survived remarkably intact for over twenty years though, as I write, is now under threat. In 1978 I attended a meeting of teachers where a presentation was made about replacement of the Advanced (A) Level qualification. There were to be new exams – I-levels (eye-levels?) and C-levels (sea-levels?) 'Make no mistake about it,' I clearly remember the speaker telling us, 'the A-level will be gone within five years.' More than thirty years on, though with some reform along the way, the A-level is still very much the major currency for 18 year-old school leavers, and remains a fundamental requirement for entrance to higher education.

Much of the modern reform started in 1988 with Kenneth Baker's Education Reform Act – a substantial piece of legislation which paved the way for the National Curriculum. One of the most significant aspects of the legislation was that, for the first time, it was not sufficient for schools to *offer* a broad and balanced curriculum to all its students, it was *mandatory* for all students to follow such a curriculum. In the early years of my headship I was exercised with the need to fulfil all legal curriculum requirements whilst, at the same time, offering sufficient options for students in their last two years of statutory schooling. In order to allow a wider choice of subjects – to include those not legally demanded – I decided not to make technology compulsory at GCSE as was at the time required. This gave students a broader range of arts and humanities subjects from which to choose. For several years, living outside the law, I was in fear of arrest by the curriculum police, running the risk of being picked up by a passing National Curriculum non-compliance detector van. 'I charge you under section 3, subsection 2 of chapter 40 part 1 of the Education Reform Act 1988 with a failure to make technology a compulsory subject for all 15 and 16 year olds. You are not required to say anything, but what you do say will be taken down in order that you may later be tested on it.'

Besides, some of this statutory education was of dubious quality. Cooking, a subject I could justify for all as an essential life skill, became restyled as food technology, so that children learned how to design a pizza box, but did not know how to boil an egg. They could make a poster to promote the opening of a new restaurant, but were unable to cook a decent meal. Perhaps that's a little harsh but I'm sure my drift is clear. Understanding food, and how it was prepared, cooked and presented, came back later to some degree via the medium of healthy eating, but by then technology had ceased to be compulsory. I recall a conversation with a parent, pleased that her daughter was not being compelled to take a subject in which she had no interest or apparent aptitude, during which she told me that, even if studying the subject were compulsory, I could not force her daughter to sit the exam at the end of the course. This was indeed a correct assertion, but fortunately not one she needed to carry through. To my knowledge no headteacher was ever charged with failing to ensure all students studied one of the design technology subjects such as resistant materials, textiles, graphics or food technology. Had an offender ended up in court and been proven guilty, what might the sentence have been? A community service order designing football stadia, making cushion covers or creating posters for the promotion of turkey twizzlers?

The degree of prescription was – looking back – quite staggering. Schools were required to submit annually a curriculum return giving details of how much time was spent on each subject, down to the last minute. A copy of my return dated 2003, unearthed some years later from the back of my filing cabinet, had clearly never reached its required destination – yet another potential crime. The document listed the total annual time spent teaching various subjects: English and maths in year 9 were recorded as 104.5 hours each, PE as 69.92 hours and geography a measly 34.96 hours. It was not just the prescription but the precision – to two places of decimals – which was awesome. In primary schools there was similar legislation. Here might have been the excuse for more potential action from the curriculum police, armed with a warrant to arrest a junior school headteacher because his literacy hour was timed to be just 59 minutes.

For me, nothing better epitomises the frustration of government interference in the school curriculum than the introduction and subsequent sidelining of the Diploma. *'The Diploma is an exciting new qualification set to become one of the three education options – alongside GCSE/A Levels and Apprenticeships. It will provide a recognised and well-respected route to further and higher education or direct to employment.'* These are the opening words of a pamphlet published in 2008 by the Department for Children, Schools and Families, the then title for the education ministry. This brand new qualification was launched officially in that year and offered students a fully-rounded education including English, maths and ICT (information and communication technology) together with *'the thinking and learning skills that are particularly valued by employers and universities.'*

The Diploma was based around broad subject areas, and included project-based learning and the chance for students to choose additional and specialist learning options *'that reflect their abilities, interests, career ambitions and learning styles.'* Very laudable aims. Schools were required to offer all students a choice of fourteen subject areas, ranging from engineering to hair and beauty studies, and from retailing to construction – in addition to existing GCSE and other exam courses. One does not have to be an expert on school organisation to appreciate the colossal work required to establish these courses in a manner which made all vocational subject areas available to all students in every school throughout the land. No matter that just one student in one school, many miles from its nearest neighbour, wished to take the Diploma in, say, travel and tourism, the school was to be legally required to provide the opportunity. Thus began, for many schools, particularly those in more rural settings, the complexity of organising transport to move students from one institution to another in order to take up their preferred options. Groups of schools were forced to align their timetables – no mean feat in itself – in order to enable the provision of all options. Countless hours of dedicated work were expended – together with vast sums of money – to write and co-ordinate the courses, train the teachers and provide transport between one school or college and another.

By 2010 the complete range of Diploma subjects had been established, just as – guess what – the requirement for compulsory entitlement was lifted; yet another colossal swing of the pendulum. By September 2011 very few students were enrolling on Diploma courses. Those that had done, and completed them, were left with a qualification which, in a few years time, would hardly be recognised by universities or employers who would have little or no knowledge of what the Diploma was. In November 2011 the examination boards delivered the final blow by announcing the decision to cease offering the Diploma from the following

September, and to accept no further registrations for the courses. The Diploma had met its doom, a year before that predicted by Ed Balls – when Education Secretary – to be the year by which it would have become *'the qualification of choice'*.

My school's Ofsted inspection in June 2006 judged our curriculum to be *good with outstanding features*. The report stopped short of an overall grade of *outstanding* because of the *'narrow range of vocational courses in years 10 and 11.'* At the time we offered – in addition to maths, English and science – a plentiful choice of subjects from the humanities, the arts, modern languages, design and technology. We were behind other schools, however, in terms of the provision of courses in vocational subjects – a weakness we fully accepted. Over the next two years we sought to rectify this situation, adding a number of these courses to our existing curriculum. In May 2009, following another Ofsted inspection, our curriculum was graded *outstanding* overall which *'in addition to having a wide range of both academic and vocational subjects, has the flexibility to provide for individual talents'*. That year we began the planning of a new sixth-form, for which we had been granted funding from the Learning and skills Council, a body which was later replaced by the Young People's Learning Agency before that too was scrapped – but not before we had our money. The proposed sixth-from curriculum was based on the extended range of vocational courses and expansion of the Diploma options which were proving popular with our students. By the summer of 2010 work was well under way on the new building, set to provide state of the art facilities for all our vocational subjects at both pre-16 and sixth form level.

Following the general election of that year, and the formation of the Coalition government, the new Secretary of State for Education announced a dramatic switch back towards a more academic curriculum for all students, with the creation of the English Baccalaureate. This new qualification was no sooner announced than it was retrospectively awarded; the students who achieved it didn't know they had sat it and their schools were unaware that they had prepared or entered anyone for it. Orwell's Winston Smith would have been proud. The Baccalaureate – the title itself laying bare its pretension to academia – comprised the subjects: English, maths and science, together with history or geography and a modern foreign language. Interestingly, Latin or classical Greek could be substituted for a modern foreign language – though probably these would not be so helpful on a holiday abroad. As a move away from construction, catering, and hair and beauty, the pendulum swing could hardly have been more abrupt or dramatic. Again, whilst not disagreeing with the requirement for students to study academic subjects, it was the rapid policy change which left me and many of my headteacher colleagues dismayed, the vocational rug having been effectively pulled from under my school's outstanding curriculum feet.

Unlike the National Curriculum, which made subjects compulsory by law, the introduction of the English Baccalaureate (EBacc) came without legislation; it was left to schools to implement or ignore as they wished. But the government simultaneously announced its intention to publish schools' results for the new 'qualification' and make them central to the league tables. This was an interesting new approach to school accountability and caused me much angst. The EBacc was not compulsory, but failure to insist on it being taken would lead to a poor showing in the school's future published results. What option did schools realistically have but to put pressure on students to start taking the Baccalaureate subjects – or indeed to insist that they did? There were stories of schools switching students to courses in geography or history and away from other, non-Baccalaureate subjects, mid-way through their GCSE programme: hardly justifiable educationally, but one can see why such practice occurred.

This all throws a new light on the notion of student choice: 'Why must my son take history or geography rather than RE, a

CHAPTER 12

Lakes and Mountains

From my first night under canvas as an eleven year-old boy scout until my most recent residential trips as a headteacher, I have always enjoyed outdoor activities and believed passionately in the benefits of the open air.

I have skied, camped, canoed, sailed, rock-climbed, hill-walked and scrambled – with friends, family and groups of young people – and led trips abroad to Italy and Spain, and in Britain to Scotland, the Lake District, and Snowdonia. Also, as a member of my university mountaineering club, I have climbed in the Caucasus Mountains and the French Alps. I reckon to have notched up around three hundred and fifty nights in a tent or a youth hostel, as a student or with school parties, scout groups and Duke of Edinburgh expeditions. A year in total.

On various occasions I took young people to the summit of Ben Nevis, Scafell Pikes and Snowdon and brought them safely down. When seventeen, as a Venture Scout, I climbed all three of these peaks successively, in a time which earned an entry in the Guinness

Book of Records. The challenge – to travel from sea level at Glen Nevis to sea level at Caernarvon via the summits of the highest mountains in Scotland, England and Wales – was achieved in just under twenty hours. With some speedy navigating, by car and on foot, starting in Scotland at dawn and finishing with the ascent of Snowdon in the dark, we achieved a result which justified the place in the illustrious record book. Due to the potential for reckless and dangerous driving, this particular challenge has since been dropped; even had it not, I am certain it would by now have been comfortably beaten.

A programme of residential activities, held in July during the last full week of the academic year, was an important feature of my school for over twenty years. Students of all ages participated in a variety of trips and visits, many of which involved adventurous activity – at home and abroad. My privilege, almost every year until retirement, had been to organise and lead a fell-walking and scrambling week to the English Lake District. As the possessor of a Mountain Leadership Certificate – a qualification earned during my early teaching career – I was one of only a very few members of staff in a position to take young people on such expeditions. It is hard to overemphasise the beauty of the mountains and lakes of Cumbria to those who have never visited, though Alfred Wainwright has managed to convey much passion through his celebrated guide books. The area is particularly striking to people in Cambridgeshire who spend most of their lives at or just above sea level and – in parts of the county – below it. Many of the young people I accompanied to the Lakes had never before experienced such scenic countryside, and were awed by the landscape, which contrasts so sharply with the East Anglian fens. One student had been so impressed that, on arriving home from a Lake District trip, he had persuaded his parents and sister to return with him the following week for a family holiday.

Activities Week took months of planning. Some hostels and

campsites were booked over a year ahead; coaches and other transport also required arranging well in advance. Each year we took over 500 students on cultural visits to France and Germany, and on canal boating, canoeing, sailing, climbing and walking trips to Derbyshire, Norfolk, Yorkshire and Cumbria – over a dozen trips, to as many destinations. For students and staff, Activities Week was unquestionably a highlight of the year. My trip typically involved 20 to 30 youngsters of all ages and was based in a youth hostel in Keswick.

How youth hostels have changed in my lifetime! As a student, I stayed in hostels so basic they would fail today's most rudimentary health and safety legislation, with miserable wardens, take-it-or-leave-it food and beds as lumpy as the porridge. Until comparatively recently, hostels were always closed until the evening, guests (guests huh!) being denied entry – however foul the weather – until official opening time. It was forbidden to arrive at a hostel other than on foot or by bicycle; I think, on reflection, that horseback was a permitted means of transport. To have arrived by car was as inconceivable as arrival by helicopter, and anyway there were no spaces to park cars – or helicopters. Obligatory duties were performed daily by each and every hosteller: washing dishes, sweeping floors, cleaning windows. And at night, in dormitories housing up to thirty bodies, there was a nocturnal struggle with the unique YHA bed sheets which defied any normal ease of access or convention of comfort. Now there are car parks, family rooms, duvets, hospitable staff, an excellent choice of home-cooked food and – previously unthinkable – beer and wine available to enjoy with the evening meal. And no duties.

Ensuring the success of Activities Week involved much detailed preparation. However, despite letters sent to parents prior to each trip, and meetings to explain the required clothing and equipment, some students still managed to get things wrong. One year, a girl struggling up the path to the summit of a peak known as Haystacks, complained bitterly about the weight of her rucksack. We managed to lighten her load considerably by removing six copies of Vogue magazine, a large make-up bag and a hairdryer – items she had clearly seen as essential to her well-being on the mountain-side. On another occasion, a poor lad complained at the end of a long day on the fells that his feet were sore. I discovered that he had trekked up and down Great Gable, a ten-mile round trip involving almost 3000 feet of ascent, with his boots on the wrong feet.

Mountain weather is notoriously unpredictable. Some years we had heavy rain and bitterly cold winds, even though it was the middle of July. Other times the worry was over-exposure to the sun. One year the weather was so hot that slogging up mountains during the heat of the day was unpleasant to the point of becoming unbearable. As a result we hit on the idea of a very early start. When I asked the hostel for a 5.00 am breakfast, I intended a pack-up of rolls and jam or some such that we could take with us. The warden was initially reluctant to oblige, thinking I meant his staff to be up at that hour to cook eggs and bacon. No, I assured him, we were prepared to sacrifice our full English fry-up in order to achieve a quick getaway. That day we had parked our minibus at the foot of Scafell Pikes by 6.00 am and, having made excellent progress up the mountain paths in the cool of the early morning, were enjoying our breakfast, three hours later, at the summit of England's highest peak. As we made our descent, with smug self-satisfaction at our achievement, we passed other parties ascending, sweating in temperatures already into the thirties. We then discovered the delights of the deliciously cool, mountain-stream water in the rock pools alongside the downward path. As the water made its descent from the fell-side it had, over centuries, carved out these pools in the stream bed, large and deep enough in places for bathing. In this weather the pools were a haven for tired legs and hot bodies. As the temperatures remained high all week, we made other early morning starts, up Red Pike from Buttermere and back to the lakeside for swimming and ice creams. One morning we were out of the hostel and back again before other hostellers were awake, having completed a dawn scramble up a stream known as Cat Gyll in Borrowdale. The scramble involved climbing the rocks in the stream-bed and ascending small waterfalls whilst attempting to avoid a complete soaking. There was much satisfaction and a supreme feeling of one-upmanship gained from being out for two hours or more whilst most people were still in bed; how much more deserved and enjoyed were the porridge and cooked breakfast when we returned to the hostel.

Then there were the years when we saw little but rain every day for a week. Mist so low that the views were non-existent, waterproofs on and off throughout the day – more on than off – and our endurance tested to the limit. The worry in these conditions was the possibility of exposure, particularly on the higher fells. Knowing when to turn back, a judgement made easier with experience, was critical; we always adapted the itinerary to suit the conditions and the strength of the party. The aim was to provide students with an adventure they would really enjoy and which was compatible with their ability; an enforced route-march, especially in foul conditions, did not fulfil this objective. So, in addition to the high-level walks and scrambles – Striding Edge on Hellvelyn was always popular – there was the option of more leisurely lakeside rambles around Buttermere and Derwent Water, sometimes with the added attraction of a return trip by ferry.

I had always been proud of my school being fully inclusive – students of all abilities were offered the same experiences. If a student with special needs wished to take part in a particular outdoor activity, we did our utmost to make it happen. One achievement was to take two partially-sighted sisters with us on a fell-walking trip. They had with them an assistant, who guided them carefully up some of the gentler slopes – the girls gaining tremendous pleasure from their accomplishment. Students who had presented difficulties in the classroom often excelled on the fells or in other outdoor situations. A whole day in the open air, freed from the tyranny of mobile phones, iPods and computer technology, did wonders for temperament and behaviour. I have also seen youngsters who have never been far from their home town, run wild with excitement on being set free in the open spaces of the countryside.

With so many students away on such a wide range of residential trips, there was always the opportunity for things to go wrong. Although every visit was fully assessed in advance for risk factors there were, at times, problems caused by individuals: students, parents and staff. A year-nine girl on a canal boat trip contacted her parents by mobile phone one evening, to tell them she was being bullied by another girl and was extremely upset. She had said nothing of this to staff or other students on the boat, none of whom were aware of the phone call. Instead of making contact with staff, whose emergency details had naturally been circulated in advance, the parents took it on themselves to leap in their car and spend half the night touring the length of the Grand Union Canal until, by early morning, they had tracked down their daughter's boat. On arrival, the girl told her parents that everything had been resolved between her and her erstwhile tormenter – they were now the best of friends – and that mum and dad's journey had been totally unnecessary.

Sometimes parents could be awkward over minor problems that inevitably occurred on trips away from home; one wonders if they ever fully considered the preparation and care that went into each individual visit. People do get taken ill and, even with the most careful planning, accidents happen. It is a very heavy responsibility that teachers and other staff undertake in leading residential and adventurous activities. Most parents had reasonable expectations of teachers and appreciated the commitment necessary to organise and take part in these trips. Their acknowledgement of this and their gratitude to staff were always well received.

But sometimes staff are to blame. One of the earliest trips I led, long before I had reached headship, was a group of thirteen and fourteen year-olds to North Wales. We had set off from London in a school minibus with luggage carefully packed onto the roof rack. After the traffic-clogged joys of the North Circular Road, we at length reached the M1 and, finally escaping the urban jams, began to pick up some speed. Passing Hemel Hempstead and St Albans, we were starting to make better time – next stop Watford Gap services. Just past the turn for Whipsnade Zoo – how well I remember it – one of the female students happened to remark that she thought she saw, through the rear window of the bus, one of her shoes flying across the motorway. 'Nonsense,' I replied. 'Impossible!' She then told everyone that some of her clothes had fallen, apparently from the roof of the minibus, and had landed on the road behind us. Reluctantly, I pulled over onto the hard shoulder to demonstrate that she was deceiving herself and to provide reassurance that her bag remained securely strapped to the roof. But the chagrin was mine when I discovered that, amongst the neat pattern of overhead luggage, was a large gap where her bag had been. Next to arrive on the hard shoulder was a police patrol car. An officer stepped out with a handful of girl's clothing and shoes. 'Do these belong to you, sir?' 'Well not personally officer,' I replied, attempting unsuccessfully to make light of the situation. It transpired that much of the poor girl's wardrobe had been blown across the motorway, some even drifting onto the southbound carriageway. Drivers were surprised to see shoes and jackets strewn across the tarmac and even more astonished to find themselves encountering various items of teenage underwear landing on their windscreens. The police were extremely understanding and considerate, helped us to recover the few items of clothing that could be garnered without loss of life and, after I had promised to be more careful in future and to secure luggage better, let us on our way without further issue. I was extremely fortunate not to have been the cause of a serious accident and came to the wise conclusion that the combination of roof racks and school minibuses was, in future, to be avoided.

Having climbed mountains since boyhood, it was only a matter of time before I had an urge to ski down them. The school where I was head had run a ski trip during the February half-term break for many years, with staff and students travelling overnight by coach to a European ski resort, usually in Italy. At the comparatively mature age of 46, I decided to learn this new sport by joining one of the beginners' groups on the annual expedition. A dozen of us – all teenagers with the exception of me – snow-ploughed down the gentle incline of the nursery slopes until, having gained sufficient confidence, we were let loose on the grown-up runs. Learning with the students was great fun and a considerable leveller – sometimes literally. We agreed together that, though the headteacher would need to discipline a student for the use of an expletive in the classroom or school corridor, the occasional use of such language on the mountain – after a spectacular fall or wipe-out – might be forgiven. I must admit that I myself occasionally fell foul of the language, or that my language fell foul of me, as a result of frustration or unanticipated disaster.

The coach journey was a 24-hour experience that would not be to everyone's taste. With a comfortable seat, a decent pillow and not too much noise from either fellow passengers or films on the TV screens, a reasonable amount of sleep was assured. But pick the wrong seat – behind people who like the sound of their own voice – or be unable to switch off from the shouts and screams of over-loud thriller movies, and the journey could seem endless. Sometimes, even without such distractions, it was simply not possible to settle, deprived of the comfort of one's own bed. The route by road varied: sometimes we travelled through Belgium and Luxembourg in order, I was told, to avoid French motorway tolls, then drove across Switzerland and through the St. Gotthard Tunnel. Crossing the

Swiss border could be a lengthy affair, especially for a coach loaded with school students. There always seemed to be a mountain of paperwork and, consequently, considerable delay. On one occasion the Gendarmes (or Polizei or Polizia: Switzerland has three official languages) took everyone off the bus at 3 o'clock in the morning for the vehicle to be inspected by sniffer-dogs.

There was one journey to end them all. In the early hours of a Saturday morning, our coach pulled off the road at a small service station – very small, just petrol pumps and a pretend café – with engine trouble. The local breakdown services being unable to solve the problem, we were stuck for almost twenty-four hours. Stepping in eventually to take charge of the situation – headteachers do sometimes have their uses – I phoned the headquarters of the coach company directly to explain the problem. By then it was late afternoon and I was less than amused to be told that the office was about to close for the weekend and could I ring again on Monday morning. The fact that I had over 60 school students stranded just off the autoroute seemed not to cut any ice. Not wishing to spend two more nights aboard the coach, we tried calling the British Embassy. This, and an interest from the Sunday Times, seemed to pull some appropriate strings; by midnight a replacement vehicle had been found and our journey resumed, albeit almost 24 hours later.

These trips were all run as individual school activities and not part of any formally-accredited curriculum. But I have also been involved in more structured programmes. The Duke of Edinburgh award scheme, first piloted for boys in 1956, has been running in its current form for young people aged 14 to 21 since the late sixties. More recently, the age range was extended to 25. There are, at any time, over a quarter of a million young people taking part in the award scheme in the UK at either bronze, silver or gold level. An international version of the award is taken in most countries throughout the world. A significant part of the award is an expedition in which participants undertake a two, three or four day hike, camping each night and carrying all tents and equipment. Although I never took any responsibility for organising the scheme at my school, I did manage to join the expeditions on several occasions, often accompanied by my faithful black labrador. He proved to have great stamina and perseverance, and was always able to complete the course but with somewhat rudimentary navigation skills and an uncertain sense of direction. He usually covered the ground several times over. For bronze level we took students to the Derbyshire dales. Silver and gold expeditions, which I left in the capable hands of others, involved more remote countryside. Although not as picturesque or rugged as the Lakes, Derbyshire is a wonderful place to walk and camp. Usually with decent weather, the expeditions went off well, the vast majority of students passing their award, all relishing their outdoor adventure and gaining valuable experience.

School inspectors do not observe trips and visits. Residential activities are not part of the Ofsted framework; their contribution to the education of young people is not easily measured or assessed. However, if ever I asked past students about the aspects of their time at school which they most enjoyed or which they felt had been important to them, the Activities Week and other trips away were frequently high on their list. It has always been the case, but particularly so in recent years, as university places and career opportunities become more difficult to secure, that academic qualifications are by no means everything. I would like to think that students from my school and other institutions that place high value on Duke of Edinburgh and other outdoor projects and activities, have been the beneficiaries of a more rounded education.

CHAPTER 13

A Year in the Fens

Our Ofsted inspection of June 2006 took place almost three years to the day after the previous visit. The outcome was – as we have seen – extremely positive, with the school being graded *good with outstanding features*. This had accorded with our own internal assessment and felt very fair. At about the same time, another school in the county, 25 miles away, was also being inspected. The outcome for this school was not good and certainly had no outstanding features; in fact the school was graded *inadequate* and placed in the category known as *special measures*. I was unaware, at the time, of the plight of my not-so-near neighbour, though I was soon to become closely involved.

One morning, three weeks later, I received a phone call from the local authority's officer responsible for standards in the county's secondary schools, asking if he could come out to meet me. 'Some time next week?' I enquired. 'Or next term perhaps?' – since the end of the school year was looming. 'Actually,' he replied, without hesitation, 'I was hoping to be able to see you this afternoon.' Three hours later, he was sitting in my office exchanging pleasantries over tea, whilst I pondered the reason for, and urgency of, his visit. We spoke briefly of the soon-to-be-published report of my school's inspection and he congratulated me on the outcome. Then he set before me a copy of the Ofsted report relating to the aforementioned other school. It was not comfortable reading. The school had been graded as *inadequate* in most of the inspected categories. In particular the teaching, learning, leadership and management were all graded at the lowest possible level. As we read through the report together, I had a growing, uneasy sense of the reason for our meeting.

Eventually it came out: I was asked if I would consider a secondment from my current post to work with this other school, in order to help bring about the necessary improvements. I was told that I would be given much support from the authority and be paid well for my efforts. I asked for a few days to consider the proposal and discuss it with my wife, my deputies – for whom there would be significant consequences – and my chair of governors, none of whom might be keen on the idea, although I knew instinctively what my answer would likely be. It was flattering to be asked, and pleasing to know that I was regarded highly enough to be considered up to the task. At that time I had been in post as a headteacher for 17 years, so was by no means a novice. I felt ready to take on a new challenge.

The next morning I woke at around 4.00 am – the kind of abrupt waking that leaves you very clearly with the knowledge that you have had all the sleep you are likely to get. Being not far off midsummer's day, it was already quite light; the dawn chorus seemed louder than ever and I rose to take an early morning walk to clear my head. As I walked, I made a mental list of the positives and negatives of taking on such a significant assignment. But there was only one conclusion I could reach: though apprehensive – to say the least – I was confident that I would accept the authority's offer.

Two days later I paid a visit to Shire Hall, the seat of local government for Cambridgeshire and home of the education department. I had one important question to ask. Was I the first person to be asked to undertake this secondment, or had most of the heads in the county already been asked and turned down the opportunity? Although this might seem an egotistical detail to have enquired about, I did need to know that I had been approached with unequivocally good intent, rather than being the only mug prepared to accept the challenge. I was pleased to be very firmly reassured on this matter. The last remaining obstacle to my acceptance having been removed, I was able to say that I would definitely commit to the secondment. All that remained was a final ratification from the school itself.

During the last week of term, whilst enjoying my annual trip with students to the Lake District, I received final confirmation that the secondment was to go ahead and the new headship was to be mine for the coming academic year. The call on my mobile jolted me abruptly from the serenity of the Cumbrian Fells to the reality of my new post – exciting and daunting in roughly equal measure. After a week's family holiday in Devon, I was able to spend the remainder of the long summer vacation in my new school. Could it have been premonition that we had not, as in most years, booked a two or three week trip abroad? The summer of 2006 turned out to be extremely hot but I did not begrudge the loss of sunny days in the garden; I had work to do.

Over the remaining weeks of August I met many – if not most – of the staff, who were in and out of the school a good deal, and the deputy heads and other senior leaders who were more in than out. Education folk-law would have it that schools in special measures had teachers who were demoralised and despondent, sometimes in denial – 'what do those Ofsted people really know about our school?' – unable to accept the inspection judgement, and requiring significant boosting of morale. I did not find this to be at all the case, and was very pleasantly surprised by the overwhelmingly constructive attitude of most teachers and support staff. Almost without exception, people were positively welcoming and very accepting of me as their new headteacher. First signs were therefore extremely encouraging. I was aware though, that much work and many difficult decisions lay ahead and my honeymoon period would probably not extend beyond the first few weeks.

One of the greatest difficulties I encountered, throughout the period of secondment, was in appointing and retaining teachers of sufficient calibre – or indeed of any calibre – the conundrum being whether it was better to employ a teacher who was less than satisfactory than to take on no teacher at all. The school was situated in a town deep in the Fens, isolated from other communities, and with poor local facilities and transport links. In order to attract applicants for teaching posts and encourage them to move to the area, play was made of the relatively low cost of housing. Alongside a job advertisement placed by the school in the London evening press was posted a picture of a huge, four-bedroomed house with a price tag to attract anyone from the metropolis wishing to exchange their similarly-valued studio flat. The idea was simply to give an example of the relatively modest cost of accommodation in the town. Unfortunately the advert singularly failed to attract any applicants for teaching positions, though one bright spark phoned up to enquire about possible purchase of the house.

There were many other problems and concerns: student behaviour was extremely poor – with frequent disruption to lessons – as was school attendance and punctuality. The school's financial management had been inefficient, with a significant lack of transparency or accountability. There were staff capability and conduct issues, and other personnel matters requiring intervention and, in some cases, formal action. Communication with parents had not been a strong feature of the school, and the curriculum and timetable left much to be desired, contributing in part to the classroom indiscipline. Bit by bit we began to chip away at these;

there was no miracle cure, only hard graft, relentless determination and continual optimism.

In November we received the first of our Ofsted monitoring visits. Since the inspection which had resulted in the school being placed in special measures, the summer GCSE results had been published. These were depressingly poor and – by the ruthlessness of Ofsted logic – were evidence that the school had deteriorated still further. The fact that many of the exams had been already taken by the time of the original inspection, and certainly before I became involved, appeared to count for nothing; the resulting judgement was that the school had made inadequate progress. Given that we had all (mostly) worked extremely hard and made some solid – if limited – improvements in order to set the school on the right track, this verdict was particularly difficult to explain to staff. *Inadequate* progress – not unsatisfactory or poor. *Inadequate* was the blunt summary of progress to date, a sublime summary of personal human failing.

The school was, inevitably, very much under the spotlight. There were offers of support from officers of the local authority and other professionals. Most of this assistance was useful; as a result we gained two excellent additions to the senior leadership team. I was asked by some visiting individuals how they could contribute to the task of improving the school; my response, that taking on some classroom teaching would be the best way to help, usually led to their hasty departure.

Gradually autumn turned to winter and we were looking towards breaking up for Christmas. It was customary for the school's students and staff to attend, on the last day of term, a carol service held in the town's parish church. Although a very substantial building of Norman origin, it was not able to accommodate the whole school population. The event was, therefore, held in two sittings – an operation of military proportion being required to escort the well-over-a-thousand bodies from school to church and return them safely. The head of music, responsible for the carols which were usually played by the school orchestra, had found out – from what source I never discovered – that I was an organist and might be prevailed upon to provide alternative accompaniment. This was a tremendous privilege: to play the church's magnificent Harrison and Harrison organ built in the 1950s and more recently remodelled and renovated. It had nearly three times as many pipes as there were students in the school: three manuals plus a pedal organ and over 60 stops. It was said that at full volume – *ff* in music terminology or 'full frottle' as someone I knew used to say – the instrument could be heard on the far side of the town's river bridge.

But the harmony of the church organ – give or take a few wrong notes – was not consistently matched by harmony within the school. There was often a significant lack of melodiousness or concord, and I seemed to be forever encountering problems and difficulties. The students were not accustomed to any form of consistent discipline – some teachers having good classroom management skills, others having little or no control of their students. School attendance remained stubbornly well below average, and student behaviour, in lessons and around the building, continued to be unacceptable. There was a barely-concealed culture of racism that lurked distressingly close to the surface, erupting at times into serious conflict. Incidents – sometimes violent – occurred both within school and outside, in a community which could not be described as being at ease with the issue of race. Often parents were unwilling to accept that their offspring could do wrong, and frequently arrived at school seeking to dispute the actions of staff. Sometimes though, parents were in the right: teachers had acted inappropriately and my role was to rescue the situation, acting as a surrogate peace envoy for the school.

But we battled on, many of the staff displaying fortitude and resilience, and a gritty determination to do the best for the school and its young people. Throughout the early months of the new year, there was a perceptible degree of improvement – grudgingly recognised by inspectors during their two further monitoring visits – and by summer the school was deemed to have made satisfactory progress. That might be regarded as a modest epitaph for a full year's work, but it was enough to be proud of – I was more than prepared, indeed extremely pleased, to accept the dictionary's definition of 'satisfactory'. Progress had been sluggish and hard-won, but there was no doubting that we had made good headway. The common perception of the 'superhead' parachuted in to turn round a so-called failing school in ten minutes, is for popular television drama only. In reality, progress in school improvement can be unfailingly painful and slow. At times it seemed we had taken steps leading backwards rather than forwards. Some days were joyful and positive with a sense of enthusiasm and excitement; other days left me wanting to weep.

But we had some fun along the way. I enjoyed the unfailing support of the senior leadership team, who were blessed with fortitude and good humour. There was distinct camaraderie and it felt very strongly as though we were all pulling in the same direction – eventually away from the precipice rather than towards it. Perhaps if I achieved nothing more, I managed – with the assistance of my senior team – to fashion a school more comfortable with itself, a school more open, honest and confident, and a school where the daily grind had become a more enjoyable daily grind. I left at the end of my year knowing that, although some improvement had been achieved, there was a long way still to travel and much more remained to be accomplished; I had merely scratched the surface. Of surfaces being scratched, I am reminded of the troublesome encounter I experienced with a badly-behaved and unrepentant student during my last week at the school. Unable to accept his culpability, he fled my office in raging temper, consequently repaying me by giving his fifty-pence coin a grand tour of the bonnet of my car.

The movement of a school out of special measures differs greatly from one situation to another, but usually there is a mountain to climb. At times it did feel like Everest, but without oxygen or porters and with no clear indication of ever reaching the summit – more Mallory and Irvine than Hillary and Tensing. But thanks to everyone – well almost everyone – progress was made. Sadly, the headteacher who was appointed to take over from me lasted less than a year, but his successor was a rightful heiress to the post and has since worked tirelessly to further the school's development, with resulting success well beyond my modest achievements. As a result of this outstanding leadership, the school made tremendous advances and, in the years following my departure, has overcome many of the substantial difficulties with which I only tinkered. During those years, ambitious plans to improve the school's accommodation and facilities were made. Finally, in January 2012, those plans were realised and the school moved into new, purpose-built, state-of-the-art premises, only to be taken over – after all the hard work had been done – by an educational conglomerate which will no doubt be given the ultimate accolade for 'turning round the school'.

So what were the myths and what was the reality? Did a teacher who had no wish to mark her students' exercise books really take them home at the end of each term and burn them in her garden? (The books that is, not the students.) Was there a secret stash of school funds available only to a handful of school governors? Did I issue an instruction to staff for chairs not to be thrown out of upstairs windows, whether or not they had children attached to them? Was it true that two members of staff had had sex in a classroom at the end of the school day? Was there a member of staff who leaked disinformation to the local press so that the school could be presented in the worst possible light? Actually this one was undoubtedly true and I had thought I knew who the culprit was, even if he was totally unaware of my suspicion. Should I have been troubled by headlines and stories in the weekly local paper denouncing the school and the failings of its headteacher? I took personally – probably too personally – the editorial prejudice and frequently partial accounts of the truth that appeared from time to time. I came to be grateful for any titbit of local news or gossip that would make the headlines in place of us. A car theft, the closure of a local pub, or a small fire in a fish and chip shop all served nicely; anything to push us off the front page.

I was especially honoured by my send-off from the staff, held shortly before my eventual departure. There was a montage of photographs set to a comic song and a video which caused great hilarity. We enjoyed good food and wine, and further cabaret was presented in the form of two teachers impersonating me dealing with a recalcitrant student. The fact that the staff felt they could all enjoy the laughter and poke gentle fun at me meant that I had, in some respect or other, succeeded. And I received two wonderful gifts which became well-treasured: a framed painting of the town and an engraved hip-flask. So it was with some sadness, though more than a modicum of relief, I returned to the school I had led for so many years – one year older but, indisputably, a great deal more than one year wiser.

CHAPTER 14

The Triathlon

Although a keen proponent of outdoor activity, I have never excelled at sport. The joys of football and cricket passed me by, and rugby at school was anathema. I have tried golf a few times, with mixed success – well not that mixed, usually very little. Some years ago however, as a result of after-hours staff room banter, I agreed to take part in a fun-run organised by the school's local community association, agreeing with a colleague that 'I will if you will'. The event, set to take place on a Saturday morning in May, involved a race of eight kilometres, a mere sprint for serious athletes, but requiring some serious training on my part. For many years I had not run further than was necessary to catch a train on time; eight kilometres was as good as a marathon.

The race itself, when it came around, involved some 150 runners: local primary school children, secondary students and staff from my school, and members old and not-so-old of the community. There were prizes for winners in several categories: fastest individual male, female and school pupil; there was also a prize for the fastest team of four. I was flattered to be asked to join three of my students – all extremely fit, unlike me – to join them in making up a foursome. I had, by this time, managed to force myself to run at weekends, gradually increasing the distance to the magic 8K so the event, when it came around, was more enjoyable than might have been expected. Sheer one-upmanship spurred me on to finish in fifty-ninth position – ahead of many I would have expected to beat me. Some students were horrified to discover that their ageing headteacher was capable of running faster than they could. I even carried home a medal for being part of the winning team – the team with the fastest three members. Since my co-runners came in first, third and fourth, my near sixtieth place was irrelevant; we were all awarded medals. I kept mine on for the whole day.

As a result of this unexpected success, and newly found enjoyment, I resolved to keep up the running, finding the activity to be vaguely addictive. The following year I came in ten places ahead of my previous attempt and, because of the kindness – or pity – of my athlete friends, who again invited me to join them, gained another medal for being part of the winning team. Two medals for running – more than I'd achieved in a lifetime to date. This was becoming a habit; where would it all lead? Would I one day stand on a podium to the strains of the National Anthem?

A few weeks later I discovered that another of my teachers – a serious and experienced athlete – had organised a triathlon to take place at the school on a Sunday in June. Although by now a seasoned, if not accomplished, runner and a reasonably competent swimmer, cycling was not an activity I had ever taken seriously or particularly enjoyed. I had a mountain bike of some vintage which had never taken me much further from home than the village shop, and I had cycled leisurely in my youth. But in terms of racing, I was a complete novice; and it was to show. With some reluctance, I agreed to enter the triathlon. One of my deputy heads, game for a challenge herself, allowed her name to go forward too, neither of us being really aware of the ordeal to come. In the days leading up to the event we sat in my office together, on several occasions, mutually doubting the wisdom of what we had signed up for but with neither of us prepared to chicken out.

I had never observed – let alone taken part in – a triathlon and was keen to discover the practicalities of the event. In what order did the activities take place? How far was the run? How far the cycle and the swim? Were you allowed time to change in between? Why would anyone wish to put themselves through the ordeal? Once these mysteries had been patiently explained to me, I set about preparing myself for the event – mentally as much as physically. The bicycle came out of the garage, tyres were inflated, gears oiled and spiders forced to find new dwelling places. A five mile practice ride proved to be purgatory and I thought afterwards that I would never have pain-free legs again.

On the momentous day I arrived at school, my mountain bike having been thrown haphazardly into the car boot, to a scene that made me almost turn about and head straight for home. Having believed the event to be like the fun-run, a community activity for all ages and abilities, I expected to find a collection of like-minded and similarly inexpert individuals with maybe a few professionals thrown in. I could not have been more wrong. Outside the school, assembled in a roped-off area of the car park, was a collection of pencil-thin twenty something year-olds with their pencil-thin-wheeled bicycles. The frames of these bikes were so slender that from front and back they were barely visible. They glistened in the early morning sunshine – at least it wasn't raining – boasting their slimness and winning potential. 'Look at you,' they seemed to be saying to me, 'who's a loser then?' as they observed my built-like-a-tank two-wheeler with its tyres thick enough to fit the spare wheel of a car.

The competitors themselves were actively warming up with stretching and other exercises. I saw knee-bends and press-ups, bodies twisting and bending in a variety of unnatural contortions and a good deal of running on the spot. In the privacy of my office, my deputy and I consoled ourselves. Her bike, though by no means as clunky as mine, was a vintage sit-up-and-beg model with three-speed Sturmey Archer gears and a front pannier; ideal for shopping but hardly grand prix. 'What have we let ourselves in for?' we bemoaned whilst agreeing nevertheless that now was too late to back out. Inside the reception area of the school were physiotherapists and trainers rubbing down contestants and providing massage to thighs and legs. The competitors were all dressed professionally in one-piece outfits clearly designed for swimming, cycling and running. So that's how you change for the cycling after swimming I thought – you don't. I prepared myself as best I could and proudly pinned my contestant's number to a t-shirt which, with my shorts and trainers, was positioned on the crossbar of my bike in readiness for the quickest change of my life. The cycles were stationed a short distance from the swimming pool. I'd placed mine close to a clump of bushes in a feeble attempt at camouflage, ashamed to be the owner of such a two-wheeled monstrosity. Perhaps when it came to it I could climb into the shrubbery and hide until the whole thing was over.

So off we went, a group at a time. The swim was vaguely enjoyable, even if I was the only person doing breast-stroke. I was certainly slower than my fellow competitors but not embarrassingly so. After twenty lengths I was the last to be out as I ran bare-footed from the outdoor pool to my bike, thence to struggle into shorts, top and trainers. Here was the first major obstacle. Try as I might I could not get the t-shirt over my head; it was as though the front and back had been sewn together. After several unsuccessful attempts and much ill-affordable time, I realised my problem. I had pinned my contestant's number, using the safety pin provided, through both front and back of the t-shirt thereby denying access to my body. Valuable seconds were wasted putting right this elementary error before I was eventually on my saddle and steaming full ahead – or perhaps I should say simmering ahead – on my timeworn contraption.

The next two hours were amongst the most dispiriting I can recall. Contestant after contestant from successive swims sped past me, each offering a brief second of slip-stream advantage. I managed to overtake just one cyclist – an elderly lady with a small dog perched in a basket secured to her handlebars; I thought I saw an expression of derision on the face of the dog. Half way round my cycle chain came off, not once but twice, leading to further exasperation, grease-covered fingers and an even greater gap between me and the other riders. It didn't help my motivation that the circular course needed to be negotiated twice in order to provide the necessary distance; as a consequence some contestants came past me for a second time.

Twenty kilometres later and several pounds lighter, I slewed across the finishing line; only of course it wasn't the finishing line, merely the start of the next ordeal. The bike was ditched – I swore I never wanted to see it again – and I began the running. If you have never jumped off a bike after an hour and a half's fast cycling – or even not-so-fast cycling – and tried to run, you will not be aware of the difficulty. Legs having moved in rotational fashion several thousand times do not easily switch into sprinting mode. I could barely walk, let alone run, the legs simply refusing to work. My movements were those of a Saturday night clubber on ten pints of lager. Only gradually was I able to talk some sense into them, begin to steer a straight course, and start the final leg of the event. A five kilometre run on a Saturday morning would have been, even for me, relatively straightforward; coming after ninety minutes in the saddle it proved to be almost impossible. But I made it. I finished the course though, like the last one across the line at the London Marathon, I found that almost everyone by this stage had pretty much packed up and gone home.

There are undoubtedly some activities which one might feel challenged to attempt but, having made the effort, would decide that once is certainly enough. I would put the triathlon squarely into that category. I came in last but one of the 250 male competitors – one was disqualified for a technicality. I beat my deputy, but only just. There were a few other women who finished after me; most of them had, for one reason or another, not completed the course at all – I was clearly an also-ran (and an also-swam, not to mention an also-cycled). No medal this time, but the little plaque acknowledging my entry was set on the mantelpiece with some pride. On a more positive note, one of the contestants – a former student of my school, and a member of my fun-run team – is now an international triathlete, competing in world athletic championships. He has trained long and hard and deserves his success. I sincerely hope he will never come in at 249th place.

CHAPTER 15

Boys in Skirts

If I were to list the issues which caused the most ongoing irritation and annoyance throughout the period of my headship, school uniform would come very near the top. The British preoccupation with uniform for secondary-aged pupils in the vast majority of – indeed almost all – schools is absolute. There seems to be an unwritten rule that uniform is, de facto, an essential part of schooling.

Politicians are keen to point to other countries which have, in their view, a superior education system and higher performing schools. Comparison of standards with those in countries such as Denmark, Finland and Sweden, we are told, indicates that we have much to learn from our European neighbours. Interestingly though, one aspect of schooling on the continent which it is never suggested we emulate, is that of pupils not being compelled to wear school uniform. The majority of public and private schools in Denmark do not have uniform; neither is school uniform worn in other Scandinavian countries. Although there has been some debate about its value, there appears to be no evidence that the wearing of school uniform raises educational standards per se. In countries such as Italy and Germany, the issue is more poignant – public consciousness still bearing the scars of Hitler and Mussolini. Very few German schools compel their students to wear uniform.

The view has often been expressed that school uniform acts as some kind of a social leveller in that, because they are all dressed the same, students from less well-off homes do not stand out from their more affluent peers. For two reasons I have always found this argument difficult to accept. Firstly, even with a uniform, it is not difficult to identify students who have less wealthy parents. These students often have uniforms which have clearly been handed down from older brothers and sisters, uniforms which are too small, uniforms which are worn out or patched and mended beyond their natural lifespan. Secondly, the now almost universal teenage dress of jeans, t-shirts and sweat tops is its own social leveller. Seeing youngsters out and about in the evenings and at weekends, their non-school uniform gives little or no indication of wealth or social background. Could it be that the wearing of ripped and torn jeans, seen for some reason to be fashionable, is a form of inverse snobbery?

When I first took up my headship, the school had a uniform consisting of ties for boys and blazers for all. I had been critically aware that, as a new young head, I should not rush to change the school's uniform policy lest change to a more informal dress code might be interpreted, particularly by middle-class parents, as some kind of lowering of standards. On the first day in my new school, I sat down for lunch in the dining hall at a table already occupied by a small group of students and engaged them in conversation. 'Are you going to change the school uniform, sir?' said one girl, bluntly. Not wishing to commit myself or make a promise which could become a hostage to fortune, I changed the subject by asking them how much they enjoyed school. But they were not to be fobbed off so readily and the question was repeated – twice. Each time I thought I had successfully steered the discussion away. After a moment's silence, one of the students turned to her neighbour and retorted: 'I don't think he is going to change the uniform.'

The preoccupation with school uniform fascinates me. It is undoubtedly true that students in blazers and ties, if worn correctly, ie ties with sensible sized knots and done up to the collar, can look extremely smart – I was to witness this, many years later and in another school many miles distant. But fashion had dictated the shirt to be worn outside the trousers, the top button(s) to be undone and the size and position of knots in ties to change with the weather. It had become impossible to walk around the school without continually chiding students: 'Tuck your shirt in; do up your tie; put on your blazer.' This constant nagging of students, who in all other respects caused little or no concern, consumed valuable time and often detracted from individuals' otherwise excellent work and behaviour. An additional problem – in my opinion – was that the existing uniform was simply not suitable for the wide range of activities in which students were involved. For many subjects – science, cookery, technology and art for example – it was necessary to remove blazers. Ties also could be a hazard when using lathes, food mixers or bunsen burners. For PE and games all outer clothing was required to be removed and replaced with sportswear; for swimming the whole lot came off. If school lessons consisted of sitting all day at a desk, the wearing of a blazer might be considered a sensible option, though in summer the said garment might well spend most of its day on the back of a chair, if not scrunched up in a school bag.

In the end it took me nearly ten years to move from ties and blazers to what was, in my opinion, a more practical and more easily enforceable uniform, consisting of polo shirts and jumpers. It had taken an interesting discussion at a governors' meeting to set the change in motion. Teacher governors had been asked at the meeting whether there was any action that governors could take to improve staff wellbeing and reduce workload and day-to-day stress. We were then still many years away from even imagining that lesson cover and examination invigilation could possibly be among the list of suggestions. One of my deputies responded without hesitation. 'Yes!' she exclaimed excitedly. 'Get rid of the blazers and ties.' And so we did.

A period of consultation with parents resulted in an overwhelming consensus for a change of dress code. Blazers and ties were out; polo shirts and jumpers were in. Only much later did it transpire that some parents had never seen sight of my letter proposing the new uniform and inviting response. It appeared that students had responded on behalf of these parents, enthusiastically endorsing the change. I also observed that, although it was made clear there would be a transition period during which either the new or the old uniform could be worn, from the day following the announcement there was not a blazer or tie to be seen anywhere in the building. And there was not a single complaint from parents.

The wearing of school uniform has little to do with learning, I suggest. What it is more about is class distinction and elitism – top hats and tails at Eton; subfusc at Oxford. It is also about order and control. New schools, and particularly the newly-established academies, inevitably started life with a student uniform of blazers and ties. In some schools, girls as well as boys were required to wear ties. Fifty years ago – for most men – collar and tie were the order of the day; photographs from the time show young and old, from all backgrounds, attired in such fashion. But over time dress has become far more casual and varied. Now it is common to see television presenters and politicians, even prime ministers, tie-less and in shirt sleeves. But, as with so much reform of education, it seems that we are continually looking to the past rather than to the future, staring constantly over our shoulder rather than concentrating on where we might be heading.

School uniform first appeared in England in the sixteenth century, when hospital charity schools introduced a long trench-coat style jacket dyed blue for their pupils to wear over breeches and knee-length socks. As a result of this uniform colour, the schools became known as Bluecoat Schools. Today there are around twenty such schools spread throughout the country; the first Bluecoat School, Christ's Hospital, founded in the City of London in 1552 by King Edward VI is now located in the Sussex countryside, where it continues to provide day and boarding education.

It was not until the nineteenth century that uniform was a feature of English public schools. Eton College introduced uniform in 1820, consisting of a large, stiffly starched collar, waistcoat and pinstriped trousers. Senior boys, taller than 5' 4", wore a tailcoat; junior boys, until 1967, wore a short jacket known colloquially as a bum-freezer. The traditional Eton dress became the influence for many English schools which adopted similar, if modified, versions. Today's Eton uniform is a more modern version of the original, though tailcoats and collars are still worn. Top hats were abandoned in the 1940's. Once the idea of school uniforms took hold, it became an obsession with the newer public schools which followed the lead of those established earlier in the century. The wearing of school uniform then spread with the expansion of the Empire, reaching the colonies but not America or the rest of Europe. So it is that, today, uniform is found in schools in Australia, Jamaica and Hong Kong but not in the States or most of the EU.

The Elementary Education Act of 1870 introduced free primary education for all children, whereupon uniforms became popular. Eventually most schools had a uniform of some kind: usually trousers and blazers for boys, blouses with pinafore dresses or gymslips for girls. The new grammar schools copied their public school cousins with a distinctive dress for all students, marking them out from the less academic elementary schools. Today, almost all schools in Britain insist on the wearing of school uniform, with an increasing number reverting to the traditional blazer and tie – which continues to strike me as most unsuitable attire. A recent photograph in the educational press showed a twelve year-old girl in a clearly oversized blazer with cuffs reaching almost to the tips of her fingers, struggling to hold a pencil to draw. This was art, a lesson in which the wearing of a blazer was singularly impractical.

Politicians have lost little time in launching themselves into the uniform debate. In 2007 the Minister for Children, Schools and Families, Ed Balls, wrote to every local authority with advice on school discipline, citing the introduction of a 'smart uniform policy' as a means of bringing about improvement. He said evidence showed that old-fashioned uniforms for teenagers, including a blazer and tie, helped to enforce school authority. Guidance from the Department for Education in 2011 stated that uniform played a valuable role in contributing to the ethos of a school and setting an appropriate tone. The Department strongly encouraged schools to have a uniform in order to instil pride, support discipline and nurture cohesion and good relations between different groups of pupils. The guidance also said that the wearing of school uniform supported effective teaching and learning. This last point is particularly interesting: quite apart from issues of control and discipline, it was suggesting that school uniform improves the very core purpose of a school, ie how well students learn and are taught. As for nurturing good relationships, my experience in life is that many bullies are often well-dressed bullies.

I remain unconvinced by the politicians' argument. How much time and effort are expended each and every day in monitoring the correct wearing of pupils' uniform and how much of this could be better spent on teaching? Also, if the argument about discipline holds water, one would expect that on school days when uniform is relaxed, for example on charity days, teaching and behaviour would suffer. I never found this to be the case. On 'Children in Need' or 'Comic Relief' days, when students were allowed to attend school in clothes of their choice, lessons proceeded as well as usual. Indeed it was refreshing to go the entire day without reprimanding any student over his or her uniform. I also never observed students arriving at school dressed in overtly expensive or 'designer' fashion, another argument often put forward as a reason for having a school uniform.

Evidence that uniform improves behaviour and discipline is by no means conclusive. A report in 2009 by the so-called behaviour tsar, Sir Alan Steer, made 47 separate recommendations on school discipline and pupil behaviour; uniform was not mentioned once. Whilst some schools – previously 'failing' – have seen great improvement alongside the introduction of a strict traditional uniform, it might be questionable whether the wearing of uniform was, in itself, a significant contributory factor.

To what extent do schools insist on uniform in order to stand up well against their neighbours, who are increasingly their competitors? How much has uniform enhanced the British class system? Certainly any school abandoning uniform completely would be extremely brave. But if the wearing of school uniform were so crucial, how come all those Scandinavian schools are better than ours? If we must have a school uniform – and it seems that we must – at least let it be sensible and practical, fit for the range of varied learning activities in schools. And in any case, how often have ministers and governments stressed the importance of heads and schools having more freedom over their schools – freedom it appears that does not extend to decisions over school uniform.

In the summer of 2011, a boy at a neighbouring school to mine made a personal protest about his school's uniform policy. He was objecting in particular to his school's insistence that boys could not wear shorts in place of long trousers during the summer. His grievance was that, in hot weather, girls were allowed to keep cool by wearing skirts, but there was no equivalent for boys. But he had observed that nowhere in the school's uniform regulations was it stated that only girls could wear skirts. So one day he arrived in school wearing immaculate school uniform…for a girl. He was wearing a skirt. The press were quick to pick up the story which appeared, complete with photograph, in local and national newspapers. The photo and story also made the topical television quiz *Have I Got News For You* with appropriately ribald comment from the panellists. A few days later – how often do the media cause this kind of copycat action – a group of boys from my own school tried the same stunt, though to somewhat lesser effect.

What about teachers' dress? I always took the view that teachers could be appropriately dressed for school without need to conform to any specific rules or regulations. A jacket and tie, for example, does not necessarily always appear neater than a smart open-neck shirt. A teacher I once worked with wore the same jacket and tie every day of the school year and – by the look of him – slept in them as well. He could not have been described as smart. By and large staff responded positively to my school's lack of dress-code; usually peer pressure brought into line anyone with a complete lack of clothes-sense. I never saw anyone who was not a PE specialist arrive in shorts. It has been proposed that teachers' appearance could be inspected – and therefore judged – by Ofsted. That might be fun: remember that being dressed satisfactorily would not be good enough.

One of the new free schools has insisted that its staff all wear full academic dress. The worst teacher I ever encountered in my school days wore his gown religiously. Just as I could never find a link between the progress or behaviour of students and the clothes they wore, neither have I ever seen evidence that the best-dressed teachers are the best teachers. But I have sometimes repeated the advice given to staff by a headteacher I once worked for. He was by no means a stickler for rules on teachers' dress, though he always appeared in a suit and tie himself. He did however rail against overt scruffiness amongst his staff and any behaviour which he deemed hypocritical. 'Wear your jeans and t-shirts to school by all means if you wish,' I heard him proclaim once, 'provided you promise to wear the same clothes to your next interview.' Now that seems fair to me!

CHAPTER 16

From Cradle to Grave

'The village college.…would abolish the duality of education and ordinary life. It would not only be the training ground for the art of living, but the place in which life is lived…and in it the conditions would be realised under which education would not be an escape from reality, but an enrichment and transformation of it.'

Henry Morris: Memorandum …The Village College 1925

To those outside the sphere of education, the name Henry Morris may mean little or nothing; but for me and others who have shared a keen interest in the development of education in its widest sense, the name is one of great significance. Morris wrote these words, not long after the end of World War One, to describe his vision for a new generation of schools in Cambridgeshire, to be called village colleges. I have read and reread Morris's memorandum many times, never failing to be inspired by the clarity of this vision and always marvelling at how his words stand up more than eighty years later.

1925 was a long time ago: Stanley Baldwin was Prime Minister,

King George V was Monarch and our Queen, Elizabeth II, had yet to be born. It was the year in which Adolf Hitler published 'Mein Kampf', John Logie Baird demonstrated Britain's first television transmitter, and George Bernard Shaw was awarded the Nobel Prize for Literature. 1925 was only seven years after the education act making full-time school compulsory for children up to the age of 14.

Morris was committed, above all else, to the concept of schools being part of, not divorced from, their communities and to the principle that school was not simply a preparation for adult life; it *was* life. He also believed passionately that education should instil a love for learning that extended well beyond the school-leaving age. To read the words of many of this century's politicians, one might be forgiven for thinking education to be purely something inflicted on children and that school is not so much a journey as an end in itself, the sole desired outcome for young people being the achievement of five or more good grades at GCSE.

Henry Morris was born in Lancashire towards the end of the nineteenth century. After university at first Oxford then Cambridge, and army service during the Great War, he became Secretary of Education for Cambridgeshire in 1922. At the time Cambridgeshire, despite the prosperity of the city at its heart, was an extremely poor county with high levels of rural deprivation. Morris asserted that the creation of a new institution – the village college – would enable significant and necessary regeneration. He argued that the village college *'would not create something superfluous; it would not be a spectacular experiment or costly luxury. It would take all the various vital but isolated activities in village life – the school, the village hall and reading room, the evening classes, the agricultural education courses, The Women's Institute, the British Legion, boy scouts and girl guides, the recreation ground, the branch of the county rural library, the athletic and recreation clubs – and, bringing them together into relation, create a new institution for the English countryside.'* Although some – though in fact remarkably little – of Morris's language is somewhat dated, the basic thrust of his argument remains relevant in the twenty-first century.

Morris encapsulated the ideal that schools should not be engaged in the education of students in isolation from their community. Rather, he seized upon the opportunity to bring school and everyday life together, seeing education as for the whole person from early years to old age. The expression 'cradle to grave' has sprung directly from his vision to describe the notion of life-long learning. Furthermore, unlike many educationalists with great ideas and passion, he was able to witness the fruits of his vision manifested in the construction of real school buildings.

The first village college opened in 1930. There followed a further twelve – mine being one of the last, opened in 1963 by the Queen Mother. The tree she planted to commemorate the occasion still thrives almost 50 years on, though myth has it that the existing copper beech is a replacement for the original which did not survive. Like the earlier institutions, the college was built to serve its community and had facilities beyond those required solely for the term-time education of school pupils. Traditionally, all schools were vast resources with accommodation, facilities and equipment, unused after 4 o'clock most days or at weekends and throughout the school holidays. One important feature of the new community schools was that these resources were available outside of 'normal' school hours.

When I took up my headship, the college was open from early morning until late evening, every day of the year save Christmas Day, Boxing Day, Good Friday and Easter Sunday. There were no gates, so the site was never completely closed. I had a key to the front door but never had need to use it; the door was unlocked by caretaking staff at 6.00am and not locked again until 10.00pm or later. The village college, in addition to being school for nearly 1000 pupils, offered adult classes in the daytime and in the evening, to a similar number of learners. There were evening youth clubs, weekend classes in a range of subjects, and an active sports centre open throughout the year. The college was also home to a large number of clubs and societies. The community council met there, as did the W I. There was an active senior citizens' club held on Friday afternoons, a mother and baby clinic and a social skills group for disabled adults. The college was home to the local brass band and to the amateur dramatic society whose players used the hall, stage and rehearsal rooms. On many evenings it was difficult to find a free car-parking space.

The activities and clubs offered opportunities for young and old to learn together, to collapse boundaries between school life and the 'real world', and to enhance the quality of daily life. Twice a week, the over-sixties came into college for lunch and were served tea and coffee after their meal by some of our younger pupils. The inter-generational interaction was also manifested in English and history lessons where young and old together would, for example, write poetry based on World War Two memories. There was much community service. Our students visited our feeder primary schools and primary children took part in workshops and events at the village college; it was their school too. Primary and secondary pupils, sixth form students and adults attended the weekend family fun-days, the holiday play schemes, sports centre activities and summer schools – and of course the fun-run. Sadly, with reductions in funding over time, the opening times of the school became more restricted, with some extended closures over bank holidays, though the basic principle of community access remained unaltered.

But Morris's model was not restricted to Cambridgeshire. In later years authorities such as Leicestershire, Coventry and some London boroughs built schools and colleges to cater for the wider public, promoting the principle of community education. Successive government initiatives have played with the idea of a wider role for schools. The extended schools programme launched in 2006 by the Department for Education and Skills (DfES) committed all schools to the provision of child care from 8am to 6pm all year round, together with a varied menu of activities such as homework clubs and leisure pursuits. The plan also promised wider community access to sports and arts facilities, and opportunities for adult learning. I always thought the term 'extended school' had connotations of enforced structural elongation, or an increase in capacity by the addition of mobile classrooms. At one point it was suggested that these institutions might be called 'full-service schools', terminology which brought to mind visions of anything from a garage to a massage parlour. Either way, the name was of little significance: discrete funding for the extended schools' programme ended in 2011 and the entitlement never became fully embedded.

Another attempt to connect school pupils with the outside world and forge a stronger link between academia and real life was made in 2002, when the DfES introduced the concept of citizenship into schools and made it a statutory part of the secondary curriculum, with a legal requirement for schools to report on students' progress in this new 'subject'. Citizenship was intended to reach the parts no academic subjects could, but was it ever realistic to envisage it as something which could be learned in the school classroom? The subject lasted nearly ten years – a very good run for a government initiative – before the requirements were relaxed by the Secretary of State following a further review of the school curriculum – the curriculum pendulum in action once again.

In 2008 another new statutory requirement appeared: a duty for schools to promote 'community cohesion'. Community cohesion was defined by the Department for Children, Schools and Families (as the DfES had been rebranded, until it changed again in 2010 to the DfE – do try to keep up!) as '*a common vision and sense of belonging by all communities, and the promotion of a society in which the diversity of people's backgrounds and circumstances is appreciated and valued.*' Schools' progress in promoting community cohesion became part of the Ofsted framework, inspected alongside the plethora of other categories against which judgements were made. But it was not to last; the requirement to promote community cohesion was dropped by the DfE at the end of 2011.

These initiatives have all partly engaged with Morris's thinking but have never fully embraced his fundamental vision, being mostly additional extras or add-ons to the traditional role of the school. Unfortunately the child protection bandwagon has resulted in greater need to cocoon children from the outside world. As we have seen, any adult who steps inside a school must be fully CRB checked. Thus it is that the ladies who serve school lunches and the senior citizens engaging with students require checking by the Criminal Records Bureau lest they present a risk to students (of what one might ask?) But when school is over, children can walk the streets, travel by public transport and visit shops, encountering adults who have never been near a police check.

Some years ago it became fashionable to talk about the so-called 'hidden curriculum'. This expression referred to what students took away from school other than that taught through traditional subjects. I can think of many examples of what students might have unintentionally learned which were not on the school timetable. One such occurred during my time as a deputy head, when I was asked to resolve a dispute between two members of staff regarding the ownership of a computer. At the time, the school possessed few computers and those it did have were highly sought after. I was called down to the corridor outside the computer room where I found the two teachers engaged physically in a tussle over the disputed machine, literally tugging at it. The language was distinctly more playground than staff room. Whilst all this was going on, dozens of students were passing, witnessing the whole degrading spectacle. I suspect that if parents of these youngsters had asked the question, 'What happened at school today?' over the dinner table, the incident may well have been recounted – a real life example of how not to behave! Some things that happen at school are more interesting than history or science and assume greater significance. My response to the situation had been akin to that of a parent with two naughty children. 'If you can't agree who should have the computer,' I had told the two colleagues, 'then neither of you will have it.' With that I took the computer back to my office where it stayed for a considerable time.

The curriculum, in my view, is *everything* that is learned at school – formal and informal – including attitudes and manners, conduct and misconduct, communication and miscommunication – a reflection of the entire ethos of the institution. It follows that all adults, not just teachers, are responsible for the inculcation of this learning, which is seamless with the formal learning in lessons. Thus nothing can be extra-curricular and there can be no such thing as a hidden curriculum, any more than there can be anything extra to, or hidden from, life itself.

Which brings us back to Henry Morris, his wish to promote lifelong learning and his desire to abolish the duality of education and day-to-day life. The village college, he said in his 1925 memorandum, *'would be a visible demonstration in stone of the continuity and never-ceasingness of education… it would enhance the quality of actual life as it is lived from day to day – the supreme object of education.'*

In the year before my retirement, I had cause to visit two schools which to me represented opposite ends of the community school spectrum. One was an academy in London – a vast, newly-constructed building encircled by a ten-foot-high wire fence which looked capable of electrification. Security cameras spied down on all would-be visitors, access only being possible via an intercom and the remote operation of an electric lock on the equally imposing gate. I wondered whether people stayed here at Her Majesty's pleasure. Once inside, the first humans on show were two uniformed security guards sitting behind a large desk in front of a bank of television screens. Not too much of Henry Morris there. The other school was a large community college on the outskirts of

Leicester which had no sign of security fencing at all. This establishment had easy access and a welcoming reception area. The school boasted a thriving community programme, an active schedule of adult education, a youth club, crèche and health centre. The school had recently been judged by Ofsted to be *outstanding*, the highest category awarded by inspectors... Oh and there was no school uniform!

CHAPTER 17

Spare the Rod...

'What is happening to our young people? They disrespect their elders, they disobey their parents. They ignore the law. They riot in the streets inflamed with wild notions. Their morals are decaying. What is to become of them?'

Attributed to Plato – 4th Century BC

Every generation, from before the birth of Christ until the present day, has been prone to claiming that the next generation is less deferential and respectful than theirs, and has poorer standards of behaviour. This may or may not be true, but there is no doubting the public and media perception that, just as levels of crime on the streets and indiscipline in schools are perceived to be rising, today's kids are, by whatever criteria, considered to be worse than yesterday's.

Men and women of my generation, the so called baby boomers, were born to parents who lived through the suffering of World War Two, endured the horrors of the Blitz and experienced the misery of rationing which continued into the nineteen-fifties. We have been variously referred to as pampered, spoiled and over-indulged – enjoying flower power, sexual freedom and the right to demonstrate, whilst having the benefit of grant-aided, fee-free university places.

Then, as we retired at 60, rather than having to work on to 65, those who worked in the public sector enjoyed index-linked final salary pensions. Perhaps it's no wonder that Harold McMillan told us, way back, that we had never had it so good. A group of sixteen year-old students I taught in my last year of headship found the concept of not paying university tuition fees extremely hard to grasp; non-repayable government grants – as opposed to student loans – they found almost incomprehensible.

My experience is that behaviour of students in my school did not significantly change during the period of my headship. A dive into the archives, the school's punishment book – a legally required document in the days of corporal punishment – showed that, back in the sixties, the cane was used for rudeness to teachers, fighting in the playground and stealing apples from a neighbouring orchard. Verbal abuse, aggression and petty theft are examples of the same misbehaviour as today, though mobile phones have replaced apples as objects more likely to be stolen. The record book shows that some kind of tariff was then in operation: one stroke for the rudeness, two for the fighting and three for the apples. Some schools have tariffs today – though linked to other penalties than to strokes of the cane – with a comprehensive menu of punishments for misdemeanours.

I have seen schools' behaviour policies which run to page upon page, and have clearly taken hours to draft and approve. I have always thought this kind of approach to be overly complex and, however much one thought the detail had been nailed down, there was always scope for interpretation of the rules. For me it was not necessarily which particular school rule had been broken, but more the response of the student to being faced with his or her misdemeanour, which determined the severity of the appropriate punishment. The courts take this view too: often an admission of guilt will result in a more lenient penalty, and judges always have a degree of flexibility they can apply when sentencing. In my experience, it was not always the original misdeed which caused an individual to be sent to my door, but rather the reaction of the student to being challenged by a member of staff. A tariff system would have a fixed penalty for the crime of using a mobile phone in a lesson. But consider this: a student has a mobile phone out in a lesson and is asked by the teacher to put it away; said student does so, with or without any manner of an apology; either way the matter is closed. Another student, on the other hand – also with a mobile – either refuses to put it away or keeps on using it despite being told to the contrary; eventually there is some kind of argument which spirals into a more serious situation. The issue now is nothing to do with the phone: it is rather that the student has not seen fit to follow the request of the teacher or accept the teacher's authority. The response need surely not be the same for both situations.

My school's behaviour policy was simply based on the expectation that all students would comply with reasonable requests made of them by a teacher. Parents always understood this, and students too in the end. It allowed for some variation within school. For example, teachers in some subjects allowed pupils to listen to music whilst working, though most did not. We did not have to have a rule about whether music was or was not allowed, simply that if a teacher agreed, students could listen whilst they worked – otherwise iPods were to be put away.

Although one of teachers' most common complaints concerns low-level pupil disruption – students talking, for example, and not paying attention – it is quite clear to me that the standard of teaching and classroom management has improved considerably over the near forty years of my career. In once sense this was inevitable: today's school children would simply not put up with the didactic, chalk and talk, petrified-of-the-teacher routines that I was brought up with. Relationships between students and their teachers are, for the most part, considerably more natural and friendly, and schools are in general more civilised places. The improvements in the classroom may have been as a result of performance management strategies and Ofsted inspections or, more likely, as a result of greater professional collaboration, departmental and whole school training, and peer lesson observation. My experience is that teachers now discuss and share their practice readily, and are more susceptible to new ideas and developments. My grammar-school teachers of the 1960's were very much on their own, to such a degree that one unfortunate master, of whom we were not in awe and whose class control was non-existent, was mercilessly tormented on a daily basis. I am ashamed now to admit to having been one of the many individuals who gave him such an indescribably difficult time. He never sought help from his colleagues or from the headmaster; it would probably have been deemed unprofessional or a sign of weakness to do so, but such was the reputation of this poor man that it is hard to imagine other teachers were unaware of his suffering.

I was always hesitant about any suggestion that the school should take a zero-tolerance approach to issues such as incorrect student uniform or lack of equipment. Teachers themselves, having requested this approach, could often be the worst at upholding it, particularly since zero-tolerance does not sufficiently discriminate between the serial offender and the one-off transgressor. Also, it was more likely to be me on the end of the phone call from an irate parent whose child had been given a fixed-penalty type punishment for coming to school without a pencil sharpener.

So what of the students? Most behaved well most of the time. Pupil surveys, in my school and others, consistently showed that the vast majority of students desired calm, orderly classrooms with opportunity for them to learn. The issue was whether the minority who presented difficulties had any significant impact on those who really wanted to work. If they did, then a positive, proactive approach was required, possibly a removal from the class.

Most difficulties with students arose outside lesson times – in the playgrounds and corridors, and increasingly on social networking sites. Aggravation commonly occurred as a result of girls falling out with each other, having been closest of friends at primary school. I found little bullying worse than that perpetrated by a teenage girl, often with her newly made pals, against a former best friend. Anyone who asserts that this kind of situation can be readily fixed should try being a head of year in a secondary school. Boys too, could be extremely unpleasant towards each other, with ignorance often to blame. A favourite recollection is of a student brought to me for punching another boy. I had asked the victim why he thought he might have been assaulted. He told me that the other lad had called him a name, to which he had replied 'ditto'. On asking the culprit why he had thrown the punch he told me, 'Because he called me a ditto!'

A disturbing trend I became aware of in my last year or two of headship was the increasing use of the mobile phone to film incidents which deliberately, or otherwise, often found their way onto the internet. It was at times like these that I would experience doubts about allowing mobiles into school at all. But no, the misuse of an everyday device is no reason for banning it. If school is about life and the art of living, young people should be taught about the use and misuse of such everyday appliances as mobile phones.

But if student behaviour was sometimes difficult to manage, it was as nothing compared to the management of the behaviour of certain parents. Oh for the parents who, when phoned to be informed of their son's or daughter's poor behaviour, expressed regret on behalf of their offspring, offered an apology and sometimes even declaring a sense of shame. Most heads will testify to the increasing number of difficult, unreasonable, often rude and disagreeable parents, some of whom could even be threatening. Sometimes it was just naivety. A mother phoned me once to ask for her son's GCSE exam to be moved because of a term-time holiday and became cross when I advised her that this was not possible: 'Why couldn't he take it the week after?' she demanded.

Some parents adhered blindly to the view that their child could do no wrong: that it was all the fault of someone else; that a certain teacher victimised their little darling; that the school itself had a down on the individual – a kind of institutionalised picked-on-ness. Sometimes, just hearing from the switchboard or my PA that a particular parent was demanding – yes demanding, not requesting – to speak to me caused the stomach to turn in anticipation. How would anyone expect a headteacher to respond to a parent complaining about an entirely appropriate admonishment or punishment given by a teacher? 'There, there…did that nasty Mr Bloggins insist that your daughter comes to a lunchtime detention tomorrow because she failed to do her homework. And how unreasonable of him to object to being repeatedly sworn at by you on the phone. Of course she doesn't need to do the detention; I'll speak to Mr Bloggins to tell him not to pick on your little Lydia. And next time there's a problem, you just come straight to me.' That kind of approach would be a boost to staff morale!

A national survey in the autumn of 2011 found that a third of all teachers who had seriously considered quitting the profession, had given worsening behaviour of their pupils' parents as a major reason for this. Around half of all teachers polled said that parents were less supportive of teachers than when they had started their careers. Sometimes parents got their just rewards. On a number of occasions I was approached by parents who, during the early years of their child's school career, had defended them out of all proportion and repeatedly refused to accept that their child could do wrong. They had then eventually realised that they had brought up an unresponsive, belligerent and badly-behaved youngster who was making their life at home a misery. These were the parents who had made our lives a misery with their constant refusal to accept the fair and reasonable decisions made by the teaching staff.

I recall the parents who accosted me as I got out of my car at school one morning, and harangued me at length because their daughter had not been given a lead role in the forthcoming school production. Then there was the mother who would appear at reception on a daily basis to complain that her dear son had been badly treated or discriminated against. When once told that he had been singled out for swearing repeatedly at a teacher, she demanded to know what the teacher had done to upset him! My favourite story goes like this. One day, a student attending the local further education college where part of her Diploma course was held, complained to her mother that, when eating lunch at the local fast-food emporium (they were allowed to leave the premises at lunchtime) a group of other girls had thrown chips at her, causing her to become upset and distressed. How do you suppose mum responded? Did she contact the college? Telephone the school? Not at all. The following week she took herself down to the burger bar, bought a bag of chips herself and threw them at the supposed culprits. As vengeful justice this was hard to beat: an eye for an eye...

But this must all be set into some kind of perspective. I found the majority of parents to be supportive of the school, and of the staff. The difficulties were with a relatively few parents and their offspring. It was just that they occupied a disproportionate amount of time. When I retired, I took with me memories of the many students who had worked hard, behaved well and gained much from their time at school. From time to time there had been letters and cards from parents expressing gratitude for the work of the school. Occasionally there were presents. Some parents brought cake or biscuits for the staff, or wine and whisky for the head. Perhaps the most unusual present was given to me by a student whose hobby out of school was shooting. Having been told – on passing in the corridor – that he had left a present, I returned to my office to find, on my table, a brace of pheasants. Now that's what I call fair game!

CHAPTER 18

An Exchange of Cultures

'In Buddhism, both learning and practice are extremely important, and they must go hand in hand. Without knowledge, just to rely on faith is good but not sufficient. At the same time, strictly intellectual development without faith and practice, is also of no use. It is necessary to combine knowledge born from study with sincere practice in our daily lives. These two must go together.'

The Dalai Lama

For several years my school was twinned with a large college of almost four thousand boys in Colombo, capital city of Sri Lanka. The twinning, promoted and funded by The British Council, enabled visits of both staff and students to each other's country and school. The first exchanges were made by teachers on their own; a small group of four Sri Lankans from our partner school, including the headteacher, visited England in the summer term of 2008. Together with four of my colleagues, I travelled to Colombo in early autumn of the following year. Later visits included year-ten students from both schools paired up to stay in each other's homes for the duration of the exchange. In between visits there was mutual contact by post and email, joint educational projects were established and preparations made for each upcoming trip.

It would be difficult to say which of us experienced the greater contrast of culture. The Sinhalese – in Britain – were awed by the informality of our schools and our education system. The visiting staff found it difficult to accept that my teachers addressed me by Christian name, were free to call into my office without appointment and were allowed, when there, to be seated without asking. There were many – much wider – cultural distinctions, but within school there was constant intrigue that girls were taught alongside boys and that students did not stop work and immediately leap to their feet when the head or a visitor entered the classroom.

The devolved nature of school management in our country was a constant fascination to my fellow head. In Britain we are accustomed to describing schools which are neither independent nor have academy status, as operating under local authority control. This is an extremely misleading descriptor, but one frequently employed by those keen to demonstrate the supposedly malign influence of such authorities. In practice, headteachers and their governors have – for many years – enjoyed delegated finance and a variety of other freedoms. Such freedoms have enabled schools to concentrate on their prime objective – that of teaching and learning – enhanced by the flexibility over budgeting, staffing, timetabling and, to varying degrees and at varying times, the curriculum. Control comes not from local authorities but – as we have seen – increasingly from government in Westminster.

The Sri Lankan model of education is fundamentally more formulaic and prescriptive, the headteacher being less an educationalist and more a chief administrator. The head of my partner school in Colombo was not a qualified teacher but – in effect – a civil servant, with a remit to ensure the smooth running of his huge institution. On my first day there, the distinct differences between our schools were immediately apparent. The head's office appeared to us a sanctuary for the great and the good not, like my office at home, a drop-in centre for staff and students alike. It was positioned on the first floor of an administrative block with a view across the campus to the classrooms and other facilities which were set on three sides of a large cricket field. The buildings, whitewashed to reflect the intense equatorial heat, were decorated with school and national emblems, and brightly coloured Buddhist prayer flags.

We entered the head's office via an outer room which was the nearest most visitors came to the head himself. As distinguished guests, we found ourselves ushered through to the inner sanctum and seated in comfort in plush armchairs. One entire wall of the vast office was given over to cabinets and shelves housing the school's collection of cups and trophies. There were individual and team medals for athletics, football and, of course, cricket; awards for the school's academic success and student attainment; metre upon metre of achievement proudly glinting in the early morning Sinhalese sunshine.

The school had children of all ages from four to eighteen: it was infant, junior and secondary schooling together in one institution. We visited many classrooms, each full of forty or more happy, smiling individuals thirsty for knowledge. The lessons appeared to be essentially didactic – yet another contrasting feature; these lessons would not have scored well on the British Ofsted radar. The students were dressed distinctively in a uniform of pure white: shorts for the younger children, with long socks in the style worn by children at home in the 1950s; older boys wore well-pressed white suits complemented by tailored white shirts and school ties. This was uniform worn by students who wanted to wear it, not by students who had to, and no time or energy appeared to be expended enforcing regulations. I could live with that approach to the uniform issue, I thought. There were no shirts untucked, no ties at half-mast and no sight of low-slung trousers displaying boxer shorts, so much a part of western, teenage dress. And there was something else: the Sri Lankan boys appeared to carry themselves with a dignity, confidence and self-assuredness that might in other circumstances be taken as a sign of elitism. But they were not elitist or aloof in any way. Many of these teenagers seemed older than their years and I wondered how those who were to visit Britain would compare with the less mature youngsters of their own age.

At the end of the school day we returned to the principal's office where he was in the process of formally dispatching the boys of the school's cricket eleven to play a match against another school. Each boy in turn approached the principal and knelt, palms on the floor and head lowered as though to kiss the ground. The principal then placed a hand on the boy's head in a gesture that reminded me of a vicar blessing a child at the communion rail. I was to see this humble act of veneration several times during the course of my visit and was, on one occasion, the unexpecting recipient.

During my visit to Sri Lanka, we were taken to the country's most spectacular, important and sacred sites. We visited the Temple of the Tooth at Kandy and were given access to the innermost sanctuary, denied to most native citizens. We climbed the rock at Sigiriya and saw the ancient city of Anuradhapura. We toured the country's new parliament, met the sergeant-at-arms and lunched in great style in the MPs dining room. There was an audience with the Minister of Education and drinks with the Army's high command. We visited the largest Stupa in the world and took tea with Buddhist monks. At each venue and on each occasion we were treated with the utmost regard and deference; we were highly honoured guests and shown hospitality on a level approaching that reserved for royalty.

We ate curry for breakfast and rice at almost every meal. There were egg hoppers: crispy bowl-shaped pancakes made from rice flour and coconut milk, cooked in a hemispherical wok-like pan and served with eggs. We enjoyed plenty of fruit, mostly bananas, and sweetmeats of all shapes and sizes. The quality of the food was excellent; it was the quantity with which we struggled. We were fed three full meals each day, with substantial top-ups in between. Any gap in our schedule – however short – was seen by our hosts as an opportunity for us to eat. It was only the tea which I found to be unpalatable: freely offered, each cup was made with sweetened milk and the equivalent of at least three heaped spoonfuls of sugar. The hospitality was difficult to refuse and we felt rude not accepting what was presented, knowing that money was not always plentiful and mindful of the many signs of deprivation around us. At one temple we were proffered fruit, cake, biscuits and platefuls of other delicacies, only an hour after eating a three-course meal. With no appetite left to us, we struggled to consume any of the copious foodstuffs on offer, choosing instead to smuggle items into pockets and handbags so as not to appear ungrateful.

On the last full day of our visit we travelled to the south of the island, to the coastal town of Galle. Passing through lush, green countryside, we saw beautiful sandy beaches, more exotic that those depicted in travel agents' brochures and mostly deserted. But we also witnessed the remnants of damage caused by the Boxing Day tsunami of 2004, when a huge tidal wave swept across the Indian Ocean as a result of an under-sea earthquake – the third largest ever recorded. Over thirty-five thousand people were killed as a direct result of the disaster which destroyed buildings and livelihoods along much of the island's coast. This was a sobering reminder of the earth's potential to cause devastation and loss of life, and of the huge suffering endured by this unfortunate island community.

In February of the following year, four students from Colombo, together with their teachers, visited my school in Cambridgeshire. In their distinctive white suits – not ideal dress for the British winter – they went about the school, taking part in lessons and generally joining in the routine of our school day.

Their confidence and enthusiasm were infectious; everyone wanted to meet them. The boys were mature and self-assured, keen to learn every aspect of our culture and wanting to participate as much as was possible. They sparked great interest among our Cambridgeshire young people and left a lasting impression on us all. Our students watched and listened intently to their presentations of life in a country so very distant from and dissimilar to their own. And whilst there was much that was culturally different, there were elements which were common, as they might be to teenagers the world over. In particular, the boys were able to share tastes in music and to perform – with guitars, keyboards and percussion – a range of modern rock and pop music.

The benefit of their visit to the school was immense: it sparked interest and enquiry into a very different culture to that of the West, especially as it affected teenagers and their lifestyles. We endeavoured to reciprocate the level of hospitality that we had enjoyed in Sri Lanka. There were trips to London – visiting Westminster Abbey and the Houses of Parliament; and to Cambridge – touring the colleges and punting on the river. In King's College Chapel the Sri Lankan boys astounded us with their knowledge of British history. One of them succeeded in engaging the Dean of the chapel in a conversation about the Reformation, leaving his British counterparts astounded by their comparative ignorance. There were also less-cultural activities which were a complete novelty to our visitors; ten-pin bowling provided great amusement. The success of the programme was due to the tireless efforts of one of my deputies, who had planned every aspect of the trips to perfection.

What did we learn from these visits and exchanges? What did the Buddhist philosophy bring to our students and to our school? And how did the sharing of cultures bring mutual enrichment and benefit? An overriding conclusion was that the Buddhist search for enlightenment on the journey through life could be a real inspiration to us in the western world. The absence of a culture of consumerism was extremely refreshing. The family was of huge significance to the Sri Lankans, and family values were all important. There was no hint of alcohol when the youngsters were around; Sinhalese adults would never drink in front of their children. Binge-drinking was a completely unknown phenomenon, disrespect to parents and teachers was non-existent and there was a complete lack of any form of teenage sexual behaviour.

It was clear to us that students' desire and responsibility for learning led to individual success. Self-motivation was very apparent, outcomes dependent on the initiative and hard work of students. The boys we met in Sri Lanka rose early, sometimes before 5.00 am, in order to prepare and study for the day, and often travelled long distances to school. Education was valued supremely, as a privilege not a right, and was not, to any extent, taken for granted. The students enjoyed learning, found their lessons rewarding and actively sought knowledge and understanding. They were genuinely appreciative of all that the school offered them and their Buddhist philosophy appeared to help them be at ease with their friends and families, their teachers, and the world around them. What they lacked in material goods was more than made up for by what they enjoyed emotionally. I could not help but contrast this with our consumer-driven, famous-for-fifteen-minutes culture. Achieving well was more important than being a celebrity and the insight into life was deep and truly spiritual. The Buddha had lessons for us all.

CHAPTER 19

The Appliance of Science

One Saturday evening during the early days of my teaching career, I arranged to meet an old college friend at a pub in Hampstead, North London. At the agreed time, I was happily sitting with my beer, awaiting his arrival. Two pints of London Pride and three-quarters of an hour later, I concluded that – for whatever reason – he was not coming. Reluctantly I returned home to spend the remainder of my evening in front of the television – Saturday night TV was a dull affair then, especially since there were only three channels to choose from. (Though is it any better, now there are hundreds?) Managing to make contact with my friend some days later, I discovered that he *had* arrived – on time – and been waiting patiently for me… in a different pub. We had clearly misunderstood the agreed destination. Today this kind of mix-up, and consequent waste of time, would simply not happen; we would have used phone or text to instantly correct the confusion. But this was 1975. Mobile phones existed only in science fiction; telephone contact could only be made by landline to home or the workplace. Once setting out –

for a pub or any other destination – there was no easy or direct means of communication available.

Aside from the mobile phone, any list of inventions which have greatly improved daily life would, from my point of view, certainly include the automated cash dispenser or ATM. Prior to these being widely in use, and before the advent of the credit card, the discovery of an empty wallet after the banks closed on a Friday afternoon usually meant doing without cash until Monday morning. Actually this was not completely true. To obtain money on a Saturday, it was necessary simply to purchase an item of clothing by cheque – M &S was a good bet – and return it immediately afterwards for a refund, which was always given in cash. Failing that, a drive to Heathrow Airport found a bank which, even in the seventies, was open in the evening and at weekends.

To describe the growth of technology since the industrial revolution as life-changing would be – to say the very least – making an extremely obvious point, but the invention and application of the microchip have been particularly noteworthy. One has only to consider the inordinate quantity of information that can be stored on a memory stick typically the size of a door key, and the impressive computational ability of our many hand-held devices. It is said that today's mobile phone has more computer power than the Apollo 11 spacecraft which landed men on the Moon.

Those of us who have been teaching for the past forty years have seen the significant contribution technology has made to schools. Before widespread use of the photocopier, teachers would spend hours writing or typing onto carbon paper to produce a master which could run off copies on a spirit duplicator. The Banda machine – a 1923 invention named after Block and Anderson, the company which commonly marketed these duplicators in Britain – was teachers' primary means of producing a class set of worksheets. With care – and some luck – the last of the thirty copies produced would still be vaguely legible. Without such care, or when in a hurry, the machine could mangle the master on its first revolution, rendering useless an evening's work in less than a minute. Many a newly-qualified teacher has been reduced to tears as the result of careless use of the spirit duplicator – a heady sniff of the alcoholic fumes from the fluid inside the contraption being the only available consolation. With the worksheet then destroyed, students would be reduced to copying notes from the blackboard – another elaborately constructed lesson plan going out of the window. Advancing technology later brought the offset lithograph to schools, a machine which saved much teacher angst, though this too, like the Banda machine, was eventually made redundant when the photocopier arrived.

My first promoted post – to a scale two position, worth an additional £20 each month after tax – was for responsibility of the school's grandly titled audio-visual aids. These comprised two reel-to-reel tape recorders, a record player with stereo speakers and a state-of-the-art Bell and Howell cine projector. My role was to maintain these items in pristine condition, a task made possible by ensuring they were kept securely stored in a cupboard to which only I had access, scrupulously avoiding any request for their loan. A later addition to my collection was a video-cassette recorder – a novel, barely-portable device the size and weight of a baby elephant. The cost of this beast, together with the single video tape the school owned, was equal to my annual salary – a good reason for keeping it, too, under lock and key. In any case, we found only limited use for the new machine, primarily because the exorbitant price of tapes did not permit the keeping of recordings for more than a day or so.

But it was the cine projector which entertained best. Provided the film was correctly threaded, did not jump or snag, and remained intact for the entire length of the showing, the science films I showed my classes always went down well. The pièce-de-résistance, particularly useful for the last five minutes of a wet Friday afternoon lesson – if students had earned suitable reward – was to rerun parts of the film backwards. Thus we saw chickens hatching back into their eggs, rockets returning to their launch-pads, explosions reversed and water flowing uphill back to its container. My favourite was from a physics film on collisions and impacts, which showed a crash-test car instantaneously returning from a collection of scrap metal to its original state as a working vehicle.

Payment for such responsibilities as being in charge of equipment was then commonplace, but the revision of teachers' pay structure in 2006 effectively made promotion impossible, other than for staff assuming additional teaching or leadership roles. TLRs, as they became known, replaced the old management allowances which had been used for a range of additional responsibilities such as my highly skilled (?) organisation of the audio-visual cupboard. In truth, the old allowances had been used by schools to retain staff at a time of significant teacher shortage. It was said that anyone worth their salt could expect some promotion by the end of their first or second year of teaching.

The very term 'audio-visual' conjures up a world that is quaintly old-fashioned, and means little today given the number of devices currently in use which create both sound and light. It seems a huge jump from the slide projector of the 1970s to today's computers now so freely used in the classroom. Early computers were massive devices with limited capacity and their own technical programming language. The first I encountered was in my initial year of university and was so large it occupied the entire downstairs of a sizeable building. The device was accessed by sets of cards which were painstakingly punched out by students and deposited at the computer centre's reception. The programmes were run overnight and the results collected the following morning – a long-winded and tedious business compared to the world of instant response to which we have now become accustomed.

Computers did not arrive in schools until the 1980s, when government subsidy began to make them affordable. The first machine I came across in school was a large black box which was loaded by means of a tape-cassette player – a lengthy and sometimes futile business. As an object of interest – if not a 'toy for the boys' – it provided much fascination, but was of little practical value in the classroom. Over time the machines became more user-friendly, performed with greater reliability and the disc-drive replaced the need for half an hour spent with the cassette machine. From about 1984, as local authorities made central purchasing agreements with computer companies – this was before schools managed their own budgets – computers became commonplace in the classroom. The period of my headship saw the number of computers in my school increase tenfold from 25 – or one for every thirty students, to 250 – one for every four. There were even schools where every pupil was provided with their own. Teachers are now routinely supplied with their own laptops; it is hard for most staff to envisage teaching without one. There are also projectors in most classrooms – digital models, not the kind that require the threading of film. These machines are used daily to make power-point presentations, show video clips and images, and generally allow teachers to present their lessons in a more professional style.

Computers have also become widely used for school administration. As an acting deputy head in London, I used one to assist me in producing the daily list of cover for absent staff. When the list on the staffroom notice board changed from handwritten form to computer printout, some staff reacted with scepticism. In particular there was concern about the process behind decisions as to who would lose their free period in order to sit with the class of an absent teacher. One individual, a kindly and somewhat traditional man, could not be disabused of his conviction that it was the computer, not me, making these decisions. Because he was frequently taken from his non-teaching lesson on a Monday morning, he became convinced that the technology was against him personally, that the computer would be the ruination of the world, and that we were all heading for hell in a handcart.

Schools' response to students' use of their own new devices is, traditionally, to ban them. When I was a schoolboy, ball-point pens were banned because they were supposedly bad for students' handwriting. Calculators, when they replaced logarithm tables and slide rules, were banned because they were bad for students' numerical skills. And later, mobile phones were banned because they were… er, mobile phones. Personally, I regretted the passing of log tables and, like any other mathematical anorak, have kept a cherished copy of Frank Castle's five figure tables which include a full set of square and cube roots, reciprocals and trigonometrical functions.

My colleagues would readily testify to the fact that I was always slow to adapt to new technology. I came late to the benefits of a mobile phone and, although I can see the advantages of instant communication, I have never sought to be permanently contactable – enjoying instead the tranquillity that being beyond range of the cell network can sometimes bring. My family too have accused me of being slow to enter the twenty-first century, describing me as an analogue man in a digital world, an observation it is hard to deny. A piece of equipment I always yearned for was a wind-up gramophone of the 'His Master's Voice' prototype; this was my kind of technology. On my retirement I was given, as one of a number of extremely generous leaving presents, just such a machine. My dream realised, I have since been able to enjoy a wonderful selection of 78s from opera to big band, and from Benjamin Britten to Billy Cotton. *I'm dreaming of a white Christmas*, sung so memorably by Bing Crosby, never sounded so good.

I admit though, that – like almost every other person on the planet – I would be lost without the internet. Email has transformed my working habits, even if I have put my foot down about engaging with Facebook or other social networking sites. As a physicist, I ought to be more accommodating, and welcoming of the application and use of the many advances in technology and science. I was, after all, brought up on particle theory and special relativity. At least I know my gigabyte from my nanosecond. A gigabyte is a huge amount of stuff: a nanosecond is no time at all – the interval between the traffic light turning from red and the driver behind blowing his horn.

So from the era when teachers used blackboard and chalk, wrote reports by hand with fountain pen and entertained their students with cine film played backwards, schools have moved – by fits and starts – into the modern world. The problem is that some of us took a long time to catch up – if indeed we ever fully did. I ended my years of headship with a fairly sound working knowledge of twenty-first century technology, though I still have some way to go, and feel that the speed of future developments may yet leave me wanting. But despite a preference to hear music on CD rather than iPod, a reluctance to engage in the world of tweeting and twittering, and a contentment to watch films in no more than two dimensions, one thing is definite: I have never again sat in a bar waiting for someone who is waiting for me in another establishment across the street.

CHAPTER 20

A Very Special School

Every school has a handful of students who do not cope with the traditional curriculum and have become disaffected, if not totally switched off. This disaffection is usually reflected in poor behaviour – during lessons and around the school generally – and can have a disproportionate effect on other students and staff. As long ago as 1995, we had started to identify such students, who were in danger of being excluded from school altogether – 'expelled' was the word we used then – and had begun to make special arrangements for them. One of my deputy heads set up an alternative programme for what was originally just two or three individuals – a programme which meant the youngsters could remain at school, albeit following a different timetable to other students. We acknowledged fully that, for these students, the traditional pattern of schooling had failed and that a more flexible, varied educational diet was required.

Over time, this alternative curriculum proved highly successful, and for many years we had no permanent exclusions. Such was the success, that we attracted the attention of the local authority who began to place with us students from other secondary schools. These were youngsters who were similarly in danger of exclusion but whose own school did not have our level of provision. There were also students who *had* been expelled from other schools, and for whom no other educational institution was suitable or available. Most had personal and social difficulties, some were offenders and well-known to the police. All had displayed behavioural problems and failed to engage with traditional secondary schooling; they were some of the most difficult kids around. The special unit grew substantially and a few years later moved into a new base – the youth club building which, although occupied in the evenings, was available during the school day. This student centre took on a life of its own and by the turn of the millennium had over 50 youngsters attending from all over the county; some came from even further afield. We had many visitors, among them tutors from the Open University who were impressed enough to produce a video of our work, subsequently used to accompany their study unit in managing students with challenging behaviour. Three years later Ofsted inspectors praised the work of the centre, stating that: '*The curriculum in the student centre encourages good attendance and is highly motivating for students with behavioural, social and emotional difficulties.*'

In 2008, for a variety of reasons – not least the wretched league tables, which were beginning to punish us for the inevitably poorer performance of these students who had dropped out of mainstream schooling – we established the centre as a school in its own right. The new, special school was independent of the village college but shared the same senior leadership team and governing body. As head then of two schools I was awarded the august title of 'executive headteacher' – an ultimate accolade of pomposity and pretension. In practice, the newly bestowed designation made little difference: my deputy continued her excellent work in leading and managing the special school from day to day.

Then came the crunch: a year after opening the new school we had a visit from Ofsted – and the inspectoral mood had changed significantly…

'*In accordance with section 13 (3) of the Education Act 2005, Her Majesty's Chief Inspector is of the opinion that this school requires special measures because it is failing to give its pupils an acceptable standard of education and the persons responsible for leading, managing or governing the school are not demonstrating the capacity to secure the necessary improvement.*'…

Harsh words indeed; words which no headteacher would ever wish to hear as a description of their school. Very different words from those we had heard in previous school inspections. I thought my year of secondment had been my last encounter with a school in special measures. But the reality was this: as part of the larger school, our work with students who had behavioural, emotional and social difficulties had attracted praise from Ofsted inspectors; as a separate school – judged against a common secondary-school national framework – it did not come up to standard.

It had been almost a year to the day after the special school opened that we received the phone call informing us of an inspection two days hence. After a total of six full Ofsted experiences, it might be imagined that I was well used to these phone calls and the subsequent visits. But the voice relaying the information that a team of inspectors would be arriving within 48 hours still had the power to drain the blood. I wonder how easy it must have been to make such calls to schools, informing the head of a forthcoming inspection. The tone was always so calm and measured, with a touch of the everyday about it. Like a call from the garage to tell you your car was ready for collection after a service, or from a department store informing you that the furniture you ordered had arrived. What might the expected response be? 'Oh thank you so much; I do appreciate you phoning – your call is important to me.' But these calls were not part of life's daily routine; they set in train a comprehensive and all-consuming process which lasted just a few days but had the ageing effect of years.

Ofsted: '*raising standards, improving lives,*' reads their strap-line. It may well have raised standards – though not everyone might agree – but it never did anything to improve my life. My computer spell-checker objects to the word *Ofsted* and accords it a red squiggly line; it offers as alternatives: *ousted* or *foisted* or, it informs the user, *ignore*. I wish I could have taken the last option. On the appointed day, two sharp-suited inspectors duly arrived to commence their work of demolition. There were meetings, lesson observations, scrutiny of documents and discussions with staff and students. Unlike all other Ofsted visits I had experienced, this seemed more like a combat than an inspection and one in which, from the outset, we were identified as the enemy. One of the inspectors tried his very best not to endear us to him and was singularly stand-offish, even rude, refusing to accept some of our evidence of good practice and of – admittedly modest – student achievement. Towards the end of the second day, my deputy and I were summoned to the inspectors' base camp – a room which had been assigned to them for the duration of the visit – to hear the outcome. Like two naughty school children dragged in front of a sour-faced headmaster, we sat to receive our comeuppance. Before the overall verdict was announced, the individual judgements which comprised the final grade were read to us one by one, each taking an eternity to deliver. Grade four was the lowest grade – *inadequate* – and could be clearly seen written, albeit upside down, on the inspectors' report: pupils' behaviour – *inadequate*; pupils' attendance (two of our students were in prison) – *inadequate*; quality of teaching – *inadequate*. In between each category and its verdict we were treated to a short pause, for effect and emphasis. The delay was insufferable; like awaiting the verdict of a TV reality contest: Master-Chef, X-factor or Strictly Come Dancing perhaps. I almost expected him to say, 'The school leaving us today is …' And so it went on: leadership and management – pause – *inadequate*; the school's curriculum – longer pause –

inadequate; value for money – even longer pause – *inadequate.*' 'Please stop now,' I was thinking, 'it's getting tedious.' It seemed such a pejorative word. *Inadequate.* Not unsatisfactory, not poor or deplorable or woeful, not even absolutely bloody awful – but *inadequate.* One seemingly harmless little word, though somehow so personal – a direct reflection on the individual and his or her performance: *inadequate.*

But *inadequate* it was, written through and through, as if the school were a stick of rock from a seaside beach-stall. Just four syllables – *inadequate*, an inability to cope with life or a description of poor sexual libido. Then, finally, the definitive adjudication: *Special Measures.* The words were like a death sentence, echoing across the temporary courtroom; all that was missing was the judge's black cap. *Special measures*: it got no better however often it was repeated. It was bizarre, I thought, that two individual words were so pale and innocent when they stood alone, yet juxtaposed they took on such a meaning of disorder and defeat. My head was truly on the block. And there was more to come: the meeting with inspectors had been merely a dress rehearsal – a clandestine run through of the performance in private; the whole affair had to be played out again in front of a real audience, with representatives of the governing body and the local authority. It was even worse second time around. When the final verdict had been delivered – the i-word having been repeated more times than one could count – the two executioners took their leave. Inspectors' departure following the delivery of an Ofsted judgement was always a swift affair. Bags and cases were loaded into cars before the final meeting so that the getaway could be as speedy as possible. No farewell speeches, hugs or kisses (or tears in our case). Just a fast trot to the door. 'Yes, bugger off,' I thought.

When the inspectors had left, I experienced two immediate reactions. The first being that I might be expected to offer my resignation. I had heard of several occasions where, on failing an inspection, the headteacher has either resigned or been forced to stand down. The second was to leap into the car and put as great a distance as possible between me and the school. As it happened, I didn't have too much time to hang around; I had a plane to catch, a Friday-evening flight booked weeks previously to visit my son who was living and working in Copenhagen. It was all extremely unreal. I was in something of a state of shock; heading off to the airport in haste did indeed seem to be running away. And it wasn't just any Friday; it was Friday the thirteenth.

The weekend was not much fun. Having forced myself not to make immediate contact, I exchanged a phone call with my deputy on the Sunday morning, calling from a café on Copenhagen's waterfront. For her, the inspection outcome was especially harsh since it was only as a result of her tireless effort and dedication that the special school had been established originally. Disappointing as it was, I had a second, much larger, school to be responsible for, one which had been rated *good with outstanding features* only six months previously. My deputy on the other hand had spent the vast proportion of her time and work in the special school and the Ofsted judgement was a particularly bitter pill. It was damp and dark in Copenhagen, an echo of my mood, and I cannot claim to have been very good company.

I did not resign. I did not feel that, although the school had failed its inspection, the failure was as a result of negligence, lack of responsibility or wilful mismanagement...and there was nothing that could not, with sufficient time and resource, be put right. Furthermore my deputy, who had day-to-day oversight of the school, was not someone to give up readily. Within days our mood had changed from disappointment and anger into one which was more positive and accepting of the challenge that lay ahead. The Ofsted judgement was a terrible blow, but there was little point in challenging it. Any appeal or denial would only have delayed the process of improving the school and taking it out of special measures. We had a determination to show that the job could be done.

The fundamental reason for establishing the special unit, and then the special school, had been to provide for youngsters who were excluded from their respective schools and could not be appropriately accommodated elsewhere. In designing the programme, the primary intention had been to provide personal and emotional stability through a curriculum which did not so much place emphasis on academic subjects – these were, after all, what students had already failed at – but gave opportunity for the development of social skills and improvement in behaviour. On reflection, and as the inspectors had made abundantly clear, this curriculum did not sufficiently develop skills such as literacy or numeracy. To establish a programme to rectify this was among the principal tasks that lay ahead.

It is difficult to summarise in a few sentences the work, the sweat, and the loss of sleep that accompanied the journey from special measures. What followed was eighteen months of intense effort by my deputy and her team. Some staffing changes were made immediately; others followed later. We had visits from local authority advisers, mostly very helpful – but some less so. A school improvement partner, or SIP, was appointed to lead us through the process of improvement and, over the ensuing months, was instrumental in helping us make the required progress. There was meeting after meeting, lesson observation after lesson observation and staff training sessions in abundance. Everyone – well nearly everyone – contributed to the Herculean task of bringing the school up to the required standard. We also enjoyed fantastic support from our governors, who had continually expressed confidence in us. It was genuine confidence too; not the kind that a prime minister expresses in a cabinet member hours before he or she resigns or is sacked.

When schools are placed in special measures there is much

action behind the scenes in addition to the more visible intervention. The local authority establishes a working group of officers, inspectors, school governors, SIP and members of the senior leadership team. HMI visit after six months, then on a termly basis, to monitor progress. The first monitoring visit – in June of the following year – resulted in a verdict of good progress on all counts. This was an extremely significant boost to everyone, coming from an inspector who was both rigorous and exacting. Though her inspection was exhaustive and thorough – nothing escaped her attention – she displayed a clear will to work with us to secure the necessary improvements. She was someone we could all respect, unlike – I have to say – her predecessors. There were further visits, in November and the following March. By June 2011 the school had made such substantial progress that the inspector judged the school to be *satisfactory* with some aspects which were *good*, and we were removed from special measures.

The school had made a tremendous journey and the improvements were palpable. There was justifiable cause for celebration, but we had no doubt that progress needed to be maintained and there was no excuse for any let-up or complacency. We had an after-school drinks party the following day – no plane to catch this time – and congratulatory words from me and my chair of governors. There was also a well-deserved and well-earned sense of pride and achievement. It had been a real team effort.

So now the school was out of special measures and deemed to be *satisfactory*, not failing. Next stop *good*, maybe even *outstanding*. But the whole Ofsted framework was set to change and the next inspection would be under a different set of rules with, no doubt, increased expectations. 'Raising the bar,' was what we were frequently told was the name of the game, but was the bar being raised for everyone, or just for schools and their teachers? I never heard that politicians had their work so closely assessed and scrutinised, or were subject to an ever more demanding inspection process. 'We're all in this together,' said Prime Minister David Cameron, a phrase repeated by members of his government. 'But,' as I often thought – and George Orwell might have added – 'some of us are more in it than others.'

CHAPTER 21

You May Start Writing Now

I have long been amused by popular and frequently publicised exam howlers, many of which – even having been around a while – still have the ability to make me smile. A trigonometry question on a mathematics GCSE paper has a right-angled triangle with the two shortest sides given measurements in centimetres. The hypotenuse is labelled x. 'Find x,' asks the question. Some bright spark of a student has drawn a ring around the x with an arrow pointing: 'Here it is!' Another maths question, algebra this time, asks the candidates to expand an expression with two variables a+b inside a bracket, to the power of three. An inventive pupil has rewritten the bracket with its contents several times, each with the a and b further apart. Then there was the question: 'Name six animals which live in the Artic.' Some clever dick has answered: 'Two polar bears and four seals.' I have also witnessed many howlers at first hand. In my early years of teaching I produced a science worksheet with diagrams of commonly-used laboratory apparatus – bunsen burner, beaker, tripod and so forth. Under each small picture was a space for the answer to be written. 'Name these pieces of scientific equipment,' I had asked. One student had done exactly that; each was neatly labelled: Ben, John, Sophie, Emma … Well I had asked!

Tests and examinations perform a number of functions: they supply information to students, teachers and parents as to how well subject material has been learned and understood; they provide a check on progress; they are used to make comparisons – between pupils, teachers and schools; they can act as incentives; they are used to differentiate between students for the purpose of setting by ability; and they can lead to the awarding of recognised qualifications and thence to gain entry to further and higher education. A student once surprised me with her response to my question, 'Why do we set tests in school?' Her unexpected reply was, 'To see how well teachers teach.' And to some extent she was correct. In her opinion, testing was not being undertaken to see how well she was performing but to see how well her teachers were doing.

The biggest change I saw in the use of examinations and their results during my time as headteacher was the gradual but relentless shift from their use primarily as indicators of *student* performance to being indicators of *school* performance. 'How well did your students perform?' has increasingly come to be replaced by, 'How well did your school perform?' This may seem purely a matter of semantics, and I would never suggest that schools should not be accountable for the achievement of their students, but the use of schools' exam results to establish league tables and the resulting increase in pressure on schools to show year-on-year improvement has, as we have already seen, had significant consequences – not all positive.

Occasionally, amongst the myriad junk emails that flood my computer's inbox, I find the odd gem which justifiably escapes the immediacy of the delete button. Some folk, it must be said, are a little too free and easy in copying material to friends and family, material which must somewhere be clogging up the works in the parallel universe we call cyberspace. An item which was worth saving, even savouring, consisted of a series of cartoons, one of which admirably summed up this shift in responsibility for exam success. The cartoons were a series of a 'then' and 'now' variety, showing how life and work has altered over the space of forty or so years. One, for example, had a very slim man standing in front of a large, chunky television set of the design commonly around before the invention of flat-screens. This was the 'then'. The 'now' had a modern, wafer-thin television; it was the man standing alongside who was now huge, the obesity of the TV having been swapped for that of the human variety. But the one which, though not a cause of side-splitting amusement, had particular resonance for me, is worthy of particular mention. This cartoon – again in two parts – showed a schoolteacher sitting behind a desk, with a pupil in front of her. The child's parents were standing alongside holding a copy of some marked test papers which were clearly not of a very high standard. The 'then' picture had the parents waving the papers in the direction of the child, angrily shouting: 'What is the meaning of these marks?' The child was looking suitably admonished. The 'now' picture had the same characters, but this time the child was smiling as the parents were directing their wrath towards the teacher, who was shown looking extremely defensive and cowed. 'What is the meaning of these marks?' they were yelling at her.

So there it is in a nutshell: whereas the onus used to be primarily on the student to do well, now it is much more up to the school to do well. Not unsurprisingly, this has led to a consequent increase in teaching to the test and in coaching students – sometimes to excess – in order to achieve the highest possible grades at GCSE. We have seen, in an earlier chapter, schools where individual students are removed from certain subjects, such as PE, in their final year of education and dissuaded from taking part in extra-curricular activities in order to be fed a relentless diet of maths and English. But surely if students are taught well, given opportunity for, and help with, revision and examination technique, should it not then be down to them as to how well they perform? Has the pressure on schools to improve their results year-on-year not led to a situation where students are frog-marched through extra revision sessions, mentored to death and force-fed with information and exam technique with the single goal of improving their school's performance? Of course, pupils must be given appropriate assistance to achieve their potential, but it seems that we have arrived at a state of affairs where students are overly and overtly dependent on their teachers to get them through the exam, teachers who have been doing everything for them, short of sitting the test in their place. Actually – in 2011 – I read a report of a teacher being accused of doing just that: taking a maths exam in lieu of one of her absent pupils.

As a result of the increasing pressure on teachers and schools to show continual improvement, is it any wonder that schools are moved to use every trick possible to secure this? And whilst it cannot be justified, one can understand why some heads have succumbed to improper activity to boost their school's position in the league tables. Furthermore, to what extent do exams and tests any longer give the opportunity for candidates to offer imagination and creativity in their answers? Have students – afraid to take risks – moved from 'Let me tell you what I think,' to 'What is it I am required to say?' Is passing the exam the sole reason for undertaking any course of study? Has the acquisition of knowledge for the purpose of regurgitation in the ensuing test taken over from a more open-ended education? Should we not be championing greater ingenuity and more original thinking? The Greek historian Plutarch summed it up succinctly: '*The mind is not a vessel to be filled but a fire to be kindled.*'

The examination industry is now big business: commercial pressure is the driver; getting young people to pass exams is the exam boards' mission – that and making money no doubt. The boards also compete heavily with each other, some promoting themselves as patrons of exams which are easier to pass. In December 2011, a national newspaper caught officers of an exam board disclosing to teachers the details of up and coming GCSE and A-level papers: the topics which were expected to be examined, and the questions likely to be asked. Teachers had paid to attend courses where this information was disclosed. Examiners, it seemed, could boost their incomes substantially by offering a service of this kind. In a competitive free market, it is surely in each exam board's interest to secure the highest possible pass-rate, thereby guaranteeing the largest number of future customers. All highly immoral, if nonetheless completely legal; sadly though, somewhat inevitable.

Students responsible for their own learning? I think not. Naturally the school has a duty to provide appropriate teaching, but current government-stated intention of the purpose of education, seems not to be for the nurture and development of young enquiring minds, eager to learn about the world around them. It seems the point is not to enthuse students to widen their interests or to instil love of subject and desire for further study; it is purely for the achievement of exam passes. And if pupils fail to achieve those passes, it is now the fault of the school. The other consequence of this is the noticeable shift in emphasis – for some students – away from wanting to perform well in exams for individual satisfaction, but simply for the purpose of satisfying criteria for progression. Thus the only reason to do well at GCSE is to be able to progress to AS and thence to A-levels. The only reason for doing well at A-level is to gain entry to university; success there could lead to postgraduate study and maybe even higher accreditation. If the courses taken on the way are of inherent interest to students and develop skills and understanding which are useful in themselves, then this is all to the good. If though it is purely to achieve a final qualification, then an individual may expend half a lifetime on a trail of totally joyless learning.

Schools now enter more and more students early for GCSE

examinations in certain subjects. This is not just early entry for the most able students, those who are capable of achieving A and A★ grades a year ahead of their peers and progressing to further study. Increasingly, this is early entry for the sole purpose of securing passes – in English for example – so that the results can be 'banked', giving more time for students to concentrate on other subjects. Figures released by the Department for Education showed that, in 2011, a quarter of students nationally were entered in year 10 for GCSE maths and English, a year earlier than the norm. Students entering early who score below the magic grade C – mostly those with a grade D – are encouraged (or pressurised) to retake their exams in order to pull themselves over the grade boundary. But, significantly, those who *do* gain a C grade do not necessarily resit, and consequently may well be denied the higher grades they might otherwise achieve.

And what drives all this? The league tables of course. A constant desire to measure, record and publish schools in rank order. Every year in August, I would be contacted by my local newspaper for the school's results. Not the students' results note, the school's results. Headteachers were invited to comment on their success and the improvement on the previous year. Photographs of teenagers shown leaping for joy, waving their results slips aloft have become something of a cliché. No one would want to take away from their individual achievements, but one suspects that school self-promotion, competition and marketing are more the intention here – some schools being better at this harnessing of the media than others.

Politicians have, in recent years, found it increasingly difficult to resist interfering in the country's exam system. It is down to the Secretary of State for Education to prescribe what children should learn at school and how it should be examined. So we have government pronouncements on modular exams – once popular, now distinctly out of favour – soon to be totally banned. Changes to the syllabus of subjects like history, to suit the prejudices of ministers. Variation in coursework requirements and controlled assessments. Constant interference and tinkering. It seems that, no sooner is one exam system established, than a new set of changes is introduced, causing constant and unnecessary anxiety for teachers and students alike. Each new initiative requires cash for resources and training, money that has to be found from increasingly limited budgets. In September 2012, following disputes over grade boundaries in the summer's GCSE examinations, the Secretary of State for Education announced proposals to abolish the GCSE altogether, and replace it with new English Baccalaureate Certificates. For the next three years, until teaching for the new certificates begins in 2015, students and teachers will need to continue motivating themselves for exams which have been described by Michael Gove as 'unfit for purpose'.

Then there is the question of selection. It makes little sense to me to compare, in the same league table, schools which select their students by ability with those which do not. Is it any surprise that those schools which regularly top the tables, and therefore figure as the best schools in the Sunday press, only take in the most able children? Now if these institutions could achieve similar results for the children who fail their entrance test, they might rightly be acclaimed as good schools. There is also the issue of schools' willingness to admit children with special needs who, however much cramming is employed, simply do not have the ability to achieve GCSE success at the league table's required level. In my school we welcomed children whatever their ability, knowing that some would never achieve the magic five passes. For some, a single grade E represented huge personal achievement, even if that achievement went unrecognised in the results tables. I can never be other than sceptical of schools which claim to be fully comprehensive and yet manage a 100% exam record. Most eye-wateringly of all, I spotted an advertisement aimed at recruiting staff for one of the just-opened free schools, stating that the new all-ability school would enable every child to transfer to sixth form and go on to a good university. Not any university note, but a good one. Surely this is a complete non-sequitur; what it is implying – no clearly stating – is that children of any ability can make it to Oxford or Cambridge or one of the other high-ranking universities. This has to be plain nonsense. I am all in favour of encouraging young people to aim high, but surely it is immoral to suggest that a school can get a student *of whatever ability* to this level.

Countries such as Finland, which are top performers on the world stage as judged by the Programme for International Student Assessment (Pisa), do not publish school-by-school tables of examination results. The Pisa tests which are held every three years, are used to rank 15 year-old pupil performance of 65 countries. Yes, another league table, and one in which Britain does not come higher than countries with less rigid school regimes. Finland, which has been at or near the top since the tests were first conducted in 2000, not only has no league tables but also no Ofsted-style inspections. By 2012, the United Kingdom will have had twenty years of Ofsted and league tables, but still we are being told that schools and teachers are not performing well enough.

And how might the latest Ofsted thinking motivate and inspire our teachers? Did Sir Michael Wilshaw, its top man, allow his mask to slip when he suggested that if staff morale in a school was at an all-time low, then the head must be doing something right? Or was that just the latest howler?

CHAPTER 22

Don't Ring Us

My first interview for a teaching post was an extremely informal affair, conducted over a fish and chip lunch in the headteacher's office – this was with the woman who blew birthday kisses and believed in the healing power of cod-liver oil. We had haddock I think; at the time cod was in plentiful supply and considered to be somewhat downmarket. I don't recall there being any difficult questions; in fact I don't recall any questions at all – just a friendly chat in between passing the salt and vinegar. Even though I didn't contribute much to the conversation – it was singularly one-sided – I'm pleased to say that I was offered the position. I would have been upset not to have been – I was the only candidate. It doesn't always follow that being the only candidate for a post means that the job is in the bag, but it must be pretty dispiriting to have no competition and then fail to be appointed. At my second interview there were two of us, but since the post involved responsibility for physics, and my sole competitor was a biology teacher, I reckoned from the start that I was in with a good chance. So it proved; I got that job too. Thereafter things became a little tougher and for senior teacher, deputy head and headship positions there were more – sometimes many more – applicants and the appointment procedures were considerably more rigorous. There were several disappointments along the way.

The format of the interview process has altered substantially over the period of my teaching career, one of the biggest changes being the increased involvement of school governors. Back in the 1970s, governors were mostly out of sight and out of mind, even when headship and other senior posts were being filled. Usually meeting once or twice a year, and only visiting the school on formal occasions such as speech days, the governing body kept its distance. There were few parents or members of staff on the governing body then, most governors being appointed by the school's local authority. In some parts of the country, party politics played a significant role, with councillors more concerned with their political affiliation than the management of the school. Things changed considerably in the 1980s when more responsibility was devolved to school level; local authority influence waned as governor involvement increased.

I always considered myself fortunate in having an outstanding governing body, chaired – for well over half my time as head – by a man with great commitment and integrity. I felt extremely comfortable about governors visiting informally, talking to staff and attending meetings; it felt as though they were all focused on securing the best interests of the school and its students. With the occasional exception, all governors I worked with during the years of my headship were supportive of my leadership and, when critical, were always constructive and positive. There had been just one individual who caused real trouble by refusing, from the outset, to co-operate with other governors or accept his position as a team member. He saw his role as one of making life difficult for the school and – at a full governors' meeting – declared his intention to 'put sand in the works'. With complaint to his party bosses in Shire Hall, and the backing of an otherwise totally united governing body, we readily disposed of him – I like to think we put sand in *his* works.

Another significant change in appointment procedure was the

introduction of the teaching observation. Most, if not all, schools appointing teachers now require candidates to be observed in action in the classroom. I was never put through this particular ordeal – it was not then on the agenda – but it is hard to deny the sense of watching prospective teachers at work, prior to making an appointment. This probably gives a better indication of future performance than judging table manners or the etiquette of eating fish and chips with fingers. For senior posts there are now other hoops through which to jump: discussion groups, in-tray exercises, and panel interviews with a range of staff, parents, governors and – most recently – students. To have been interviewed by school pupils thirty years ago would have been unheard of – unprofessional even – not unlike allowing the lunatics to run the asylum. But students can be extremely perceptive, rigorous in questioning and not always bound by social norms and niceties. With guidance and training, they can make a constructive contribution to the appointment of the individuals who will end up teaching them.

A further change in the selection process was the move towards allowing candidates to return home after their final interview, contacting them later by phone to confirm success or otherwise. This had not always been standard procedure. For every interview to which I was called, candidates were required to wait around before being informed of the decision. In one of the London Boroughs in which I worked, there was an education officer, present at secondary school interviews for senior positions, whose function was to carry the news to the awaiting ensemble. I encountered her twice. She would enter the room where candidates had been patiently waiting, smiling at everyone – had we all been successful perhaps? Her manner and visage appeared to indicate that we had. But no, with the announcement of the name of the successful candidate – on one occasion, me – who then followed her back to the interview room, she turned to give the rest of the group a broad grin. She evidently revelled in this role. 'The hatchet woman,' we called her.

One advantage of keeping candidates waiting for the outcome of an interview was that it allowed an opportunity to offer a debrief to the unsuccessful applicants. Delivering this feedback could be difficult, especially to a candidate who had performed poorly. How much easier it would have been to simply say: 'I'm so terribly sorry; although you interviewed extremely well, you were just pipped to the post.' Telling the truth was more painful. I once told a disappointed contender for a deputy position that he had come across as over-assertive and somewhat aggressive. This had been the genuine and honest conclusion of the interview panel. At this, he flew into a vituperative rage, said I had no idea what I was talking about, and informed me that we had made a serious error in not appointing him. This merely confirmed my opinion that the serious error would have been to *have* appointed him. He simply refused to accept the unwelcome decision. I almost expected to be told that we would be hearing from his solicitors. On another occasion I had to inform a timid, luckless individual – who was at the other end of the belligerence spectrum – that he appeared in the interview to be indecisive and rather wishy-washy. Did he accept this reasoning for not appointing him? 'Maybe,' he told me, 'but then again maybe not.'

I wonder how many times the question has been asked at interview: 'What would you say were your strengths?' It is a question that invites so many imaginative responses. 'I am Superman, can fly from planet to planet, and have many times saved the world,' should be a pretty persuasive answer, as might be the disclosure of possessing x-ray vision or more than one brain. 'I am an outstanding teacher and leader, have taught dumb animals to read and write and have never made an error of judgement or mistake of any kind,' could similarly impress, or at least provide material for discussion. Equally there is the question, 'What do you think is your biggest weakness?' How on earth is one supposed to answer that? 'My weakness is that I am totally incompetent,' would probably sink you on the spot, as would an admission that you were an organised drug dealer or a serial killer on the run. Of course the trick with this one is to answer by making a virtue out of a vice: 'I am excessively conscientious and have often been told that I work too hard,' might sway any jury, as could, 'I am sometimes too tolerant of other people.' One might be tempted to respond to this particular question with the comeback: 'My weakness is that I am too inclined to treat questions like that seriously.'

In 1988 I had an interview for a deputy headship, part of which involved the candidates in a discussion on a current educational topic. The debate was observed by the head, other deputies and a local authority officer, each of whom sat in a corner of the room with clip-board and pen. I spent the session – which seemed an eternity – carefully considering my input. It was clear that we were being scrutinised, not so much for the content of our individual contributions, but more for the manner and style of our delivery. One candidate leapt in immediately with an over-confident and almost objectionable opinion. 'That's him out,' I thought as I timed carefully my entry into the conversation. One candidate said nothing at all throughout the process; I couldn't see how that could have helped his prospects. The whole affair was played out as something of a game – Monopoly perhaps, or Snakes and Ladders; only missing were the dice. My verbal skills – or should I say my skill of verbosity – served me well and, although I retained not even the slightest notion of what I had contributed, I found myself through to the last round. The final interview for this post was a singularly unusual affair, conducted in the town hall rather than the school – an indication of the then significance of the local authority. When my turn came, I entered a huge room, almost the size of the council chamber, where no fewer than fifteen individuals were seated formally behind tables arranged in the shape of a horseshoe. I had a solitary chair at the epicentre. One by one each officer, governor – there were a couple – and the head asked a single question. The same question, I later learned, to each candidate. There were neither follow-up questions nor discussion of any kind. I was also told that each member of the panel scored individual candidates on how well or otherwise their question was answered. The scores were then totalled and the candidate with the highest was offered the position. More like Mastermind than a professional interview I thought. Sour grapes you may well say, since I had not been the one with the highest score. I always did better at board games.

Interviews for head and deputy posts were usually held over two days. Until recently it was common – on the afternoon or evening of the first day – to attend an informal tea or drinks party to which were invited the great and the good. Informal? Not likely! It was death by shortbread or vol-au-vent, Earl Grey or Tio Pepe; there might have been a lukewarm glass of white wine if you were lucky. Whatever the refreshment, these were always quite gruesome events. I'm not sure which was the more insufferable: being on the receiving end – fielding the same questions from different governors, staff and other well-meaning individuals; or doing the rounds oneself as part of the appointment panel, initiating a similar discussion up to as many as eight times. As a candidate, one was conscious that after the event – when all the contestants had retired – the assembled throng would be able to indulge in a good gossip. Whether or not this circus event ever had any real influence on the final decision is hard to say – I think I preferred the fish and chip take-away. Fortunately, the cocktail party event eventually fell out of favour, probably for health and safety reasons – health of the candidates that is – and ceased to be part of appointment procedures. I cannot say I was sorry.

As time progressed, political correctness began to creep into the selection process. In order to avoid any possibility of gender bias, initials replaced first names on some application forms – request for 'marital status' had gone out with the ark. Similarly, in an attempt to avoid age discrimination, there became no requirement to give a date of birth. These measures always struck me as rather pointless, since candidates usually included a CV helpfully containing this very information. Also, the same application form asked for details – including dates – of qualifications and previous employment, together with reasons for leaving. The dates when an applicant achieved GCSE or A-level qualifications were always a giveaway of their likely age; dates of O-levels – abolished in 1988 – especially so. And dates of maternity leave gave a pretty solid clue to distinguishing, should one wish to, the men from the women.

I estimate that I interviewed some 400 candidates during my headship years and made over 100 appointments. That's a lot of interviews. The most difficult ones were those where there was an unsuccessful internal candidate. In all such cases I was encouraged by how individuals – although naturally disappointed – accepted the decision without any form of bitterness or resentment. With head held high they continued with the quality of teaching, managing and leading which had secured their place at the final interview in the first place. Then again – just once – a candidate who failed to be appointed to a promoted post descended into a permanent sulk, refused totally to accept the decision of the interviewing panel, and proceeded to lodge a formal grievance against me and the entire school leadership team. To me this behaviour only confirmed that the correct decision had been made.

When the time came about, the process of appointing my successor was an interesting, if uncomfortable, one. Having announced my retirement and had my notice to leave accepted, a sub-group of governors met to plan every aspect of securing a new headteacher – from drafting the job specification to organising the interviews. By the time the headship was advertised, it was too late to change my mind; no decision I had ever made felt more incapable of retraction. I kept myself apart from the detail of the process, though it was hard to ignore what was going on. In September of my final term, a short-listed group of eight candidates assembled for the two-day ordeal and performed to various audiences. These included teaching and non-teaching staff, governors and two groups of extremely astute students. There was no sherry party. In the early evening of the second day the full governing body assembled to ratify the appointment and confirm my successor. Even less going back now. The highly satisfying outcome for me – and for the school – was that the final decision had been unanimous and it was agreed by all that the very best person had been appointed.

As headteacher I was replaceable – and would soon be replaced. It had been a very long 48 hours, and I was left feeling a mixture of sadness and relief. But this was not the time for introspection or thoughts of how I might be missed; no one is indispensable, least of all me. As Charles de Gaulle – founding president of France's Fifth Republic – once famously declared: *'The graveyards are full of indispensable men.'*

CHAPTER 23

Making Sense of it All

The journalist and broadcaster James Naughtie has, on more than one occasion, introduced his Radio Four listeners to the idea of a law of reverse intentions. According to this law, which Naughtie applies in particular to the words of politicians, if the exact opposite of a statement is plainly nonsense, then the statement itself is unlikely to be worth making in the first place. Thus, for example, the announcement by a would-be Member of Parliament that he or she believes firmly in a successful future for the country is clearly of the not-worth-making variety, since – presumably – nobody would wish for the opposite. One can have great fun with this law, reducing much of what is uttered publicly to the simply meaningless. Applied to the pronouncements of many MPs, but especially to parliamentary candidates during an election campaign, a great deal that is spoken falls easily into the same category: 'I believe that criminals should be punished.' (Criminals should be rewarded or let off scot-free?) 'Education is of vital importance.' (Education is a waste of time?) And so on.

In recent times, when schools have found the need to become more commercially orientated, there has been a substantial increase in the use of slogans for quick and easy description. No more the Latin school motto – though a few do still exist; in have come the pithy slogans which, in the style of an advertisement, describe a school to the world in one line. But although they seek to promote worth and virtue, many of these schools' catch-phrases fall foul of Naughtie's law and are subsequently, therefore, of dubious value.

A quick glance at the situations-vacant pages of the education press offers many examples of schools which proudly promote themselves with a well-intended, but ultimately pointless statement. 'Developing today's students for tomorrow,' proudly boasts an institution in the south of England, but would the school seriously consider developing students for yesterday? So they go on: 'Building for success'…. (building for failure?) 'Working together to be the best'…. (to be the worst?) 'Where every child has an exciting future'…. (has a dreary, humdrum fate to look forward to?)

Slogans and catch-phrases are everywhere: *believe in better, emotion in motion, every little bit hurts* – OK I made that last one up. One of the national examination boards carries the line: 'advancing learning, changing lives', but without saying whether the change is for better or for worse. If you wish to create your own catch-phrase there is an online slogan generator which is able to do just that; type in any name, be it a product or a school, and the generator will sloganize (sic) it for you. One of my favourites – again from a school – is: 'A new horizon dawns' which seems to conjure up the image of the school as a ship sailing boldly towards the edge of a flat Earth.

A game to pass the time on a lengthy car journey, is to spot interesting, unusual or plain silly slogans that appear on vans and lorries, where the need for an advertising one-liner appears to be increasingly necessary. Many are without meaning or sense. It is hard to believe that I once saw, on the side of a large truck carrying bottled water, the strap-line: 'Water with integrity.' What on earth could that possibly mean? What it did mean, was that this was a situation in which the law of reverse intentions did not apply: surely most water has no integrity at all!

Sifting through verbal garbage has been a personal mission for me during my years as a head. As one wades through the mass of hyperbole thrown at headteachers and their schools, the filtering out of the utterly pointless – and often condescending – literature becomes a necessary, and time-consuming activity. Page upon page of well-meaning but jargon-ridden education-speak can sometimes yield nuggets of wisdom, but usually there is a need to look very hard. Teachers themselves are often to blame; I have read countless letters of application which, as examples of the law of reverse intentions, do no more that simply state the obvious. A pound for each time I have read that a candidate believed all children should reach their potential… (No child should reach their potential?) might have enabled me to retire a year earlier. I fully appreciate people wishing to impress on me that they are committed to success; perhaps some are committed to failure, but I have yet to meet them.

As students of language will tell you, word meaning and usage change continually. The dictionary now accepts the word 'access' as a verb, as in 'to access information' rather than just the noun it had been for previous centuries. Films now 'premiere', television series 'conclude' and trains 'terminate'; witness the railway guard's announcement that 'this train will terminate at St Pancras' which would seem to suggest either the presence of some kind of fatal illness, or the need for passengers to exit swiftly before spontaneous combustion of the rolling stock.

Meanwhile, back at the chalk-face, we have already witnessed the effect of deflation on educational language, such that *excellent* now means *good*, *good* means *satisfactory* and *satisfactory* means *not good enough*. No less a person than the Prime Minister, David Cameron has been quoted as saying *'Just good enough is frankly not good enough.'* The 'satisfactory' conundrum has now been solved – once and for all – by the simple act of abolishing the term as it applies to school inspection. Prior to this, satisfactory schools had been threatened with being placed in special measures if they did not reach the 'good' category within three years. At the time, the Ofsted inspection framework stated that for schools to be rated 'good', standards should be broadly at or above national average; being below average was not acceptable. So here was another piece of nonsense: the requirement for all schools to be at least average. But of course, if there are to be schools above average, there will always be schools below average.

Politicians and the media had sometimes grouped schools, as a result of Ofsted inspections, into two broad categories. In the summer of 2010 a junior education minister, referring to schools recently inspected, bemoaned the fact that almost half had been judged satisfactory or inadequate, with just over fifty percent good or outstanding. Surely this was disingenuous to say the least; all headteachers work hard to improve their schools, but the plain fact is, that in drawing a line which placed satisfactory on the same side as inadequate, the clear impression given was that satisfactory was – once again – simply not good enough. Ofsted's own figures show that, of the schools inspected between September 2009 and March 2010, 11% were outstanding, 42% were good and 38% satisfactory. In other words over 90% of schools were judged to be satisfactory or better. I know from my own experience, given the immense work and effort involved in moving a school from inadequate to satisfactory, that the achievement of a satisfactory grading was not to be belittled. Is it now the case that, with satisfactory no longer good enough, we will see a shifting upwards of the categories, with new boundaries introduced? Perhaps there might be a starred grade introduced at the top end to separate the very best performing schools from the 'merely outstanding'!

The late Ted Wragg, academic and educationalist, who wrote regularly for the Times Education Supplement (TES) until his untimely death in 2005, was adept at highlighting nonsense and cutting through the mire of education-speak. He championed the role of teachers as dedicated professionals who suffered from bureaucracy and excessive accountability, and was able – with humour and satire – to gently ridicule the seemingly never-ending edicts which were disseminated by our political masters. He argued that governments – both Labour and Conservative – should treat education as a public service rather than as a commodity to be traded, and halt the practice of deluging teachers with a language of managerialism and marketing. Wragg's weekly lampooning of the education hierarchy on the back page of the TES, together with his relentless war on gobbledygook, was a source of amusement to many. Often his column was the first section of the paper to be read.

In the look-out for education and school nonsense, I cannot omit an example, brought to my attention by a friend, from a school which her children once attended. As a result of an inspection which required the teaching day to be lengthened, the school proposed increasing teaching time by ten minutes. The headteacher wrote to parents explaining the changes. My friend thought it was brilliant: the intention was to increase each of the eight lessons and two registration periods by one minute each – an extra ten minutes in total. The new timings gave a morning registration from 8.50 to 9.01. Period 1 – after assembly – was from 9.16 to 9.52 and so it continued through the whole morning and afternoon. Lesson 5 started at 1.01 and finished at 1.37; afternoon break was from 2.13 to 2.28 – 'Don't you know you're late boy; it's gone 2.29!' – the whole thing reading more like a railway timetable than a programme for the school day. She was on the point of writing to congratulate the head on his hilarious send up – 'If they want ten minutes more I'll give them ten minutes more!' – when she realised to her dismay that he was entirely serious. The new timetable became a reality and every student was required to put an expensively accurate wrist-watch on their Christmas list.

Ted Wragg was also keen to ridicule political correctness which, like health and safety, had become a butt for commentators and the public at large. Committee chairmen have been chairs for a long time, albeit with two legs rather than four; bin-men are now refuse operatives and the lollipop man or lady has become a school pedestrian crossing supervisor. The job titles get ever more pretentious. I once heard a lift engineer referred to as a vertical transport consultant. It must surely be right to modify word usage in order to eschew stereotypes and language which in any way cause offence but, if we are to avoid the tendency towards disorder that physicists call increasing entropy, there is surely a need to safeguard against the over-zealous, ever-extending reach of unnecessary political correctness. The kind of PC which sees Guy Fawkes Night become a 'change of seasons extravaganza' and Christmas recast as 'Winterval' in a supposed desire to avoid upsetting anyone. Even poor Thomas the Tank Engine has not escaped; he had to surrender his Christmas tree in order, so we were told, to make his books more accessible to a wider audience.

So there it is. Separating the sense from the nonsense can be an almost full-time occupation, and the ability to steer a course through the minefield of drivel is a necessary attribute of today's headteachers. There is still a lot of common sense about and much wisdom to be found, but sometimes you have to search hard to find it, hidden as it is amongst the balderdash. In the end – to use the old cliché – fact is stranger than fiction; or as Ted Wragg would have said: *'You couldn't make this stuff up.'*

CHAPTER 24

Another Brick in the Wall

'Education is what remains after one has forgotten what has been learned at school.'

Albert Einstein

In 1986 I was fortunate to attend a series of lectures at the Institute of Education in Bloomsbury, London. Among the many presentations was a lively and engaging talk on education in the independent sector by the headmaster of one of the country's leading public schools. As well as his obvious enthusiasm for independent schooling, was the assertion that schools like his were not elite and that the fees charged were by no means extortionate. He had gone on to suggest that if working or middle class parents were prepared to sacrifice their video recorders and foreign holidays – I recall the words distinctly – they could readily afford private education for their children.

The significance of this statement – just a single sentence buried within an hour's address – did not immediately strike home. It was only later, whilst walking back from the Institute to the underground, that I began to work out the arithmetic. At the time, fees for this particular public school were around £3000 per term: to educate two children would have cost £18,000 every year. The average salary in Britain was then around £12,000 before tax and other deductions. By the time I reached the station I had concluded that, even in a two-income family, for parents of average means to afford such an education for their children, it would not be a question of giving up video recorders and foreign holidays, but more a matter of giving up paying the mortgage or putting food on the table.

Naturally the school had been most appealingly presented – a place to which every parent might wish to send their children: small class sizes, well-qualified teachers, outstanding facilities for sports, art and music which complemented an astounding range of extra-curricular activities. And an almost unbelievably astonishing record of student success. This was schooling of the highest order. Within the state sector, there were also many schools with excellent teachers and first-rate facilities. But equally there were schools with inadequate buildings and limited resources which struggled to appoint teachers at all. As my underground train rattled southwards deep below the metropolis, I reflected that the country's education provision was, if not wantonly unfair, certainly unequal, with a sizeable gap, not just between the provision by private and state sectors, but also within the state sector itself.

The relationship between state schools and their private cousins is an interesting one. Many of England's private schools are called public schools. This idiosyncrasy is somewhat confusing, particularly to people from abroad, the usage of the word 'public' being in direct opposition to what one might expect. Public libraries and public swimming pools, for example, do not conjure up a notion of exclusivity; in fact they suggest exactly the opposite – open to all. In Scotland, a public school is a state school; in the United

States any government-run school would be called a public school. The term 'public' in the English school system was adopted first by Eton College, to denote that the school was open to the paying public rather than – in the case of a church school – only open to members with religious affiliations.

The country's top public schools do not serve their local community, taking students instead from far and wide, unlike their state counterparts which mostly draw from their immediate neighbourhood. Living in Harrow-on-the-Hill, for example, would not entitle you to send your children to Harrow School, any more than living in Oxford confers the right to a local university education. Although parents may express a preference for which public school they would like their children to attend, the essential process is one in which the school chooses its pupils – not the other way around – selection being by way of interview, entrance exam or other means. For state schools – particularly those not fully subscribed – things are very different; it can be very much the parent, on behalf of the child, who does the choosing. But such choice can only be achieved in areas or schools where there is surplus capacity: no spare places or 'empty desks' means little or no parental choice. Unless every school has vacancies – something that could never be economically justified – there can never be a completely free choice. This is the single biggest flaw in the doctrine of parental choice, a doctrine which has long been a powerful rallying cry for politicians.

Then there is the notion of exclusivity. Like the 'best' restaurants and the 'best' clubs, where nobody can walk in off the street, the 'best' schools do not let in just anyone. The harder it is to gain entry, the more desirable entry becomes. Some of the country's most prestigious state schools are church schools with long waiting lists and strict criteria for religious belief. So we witness the ludicrous situation of parents attending morning Eucharist for the sole purpose (soul purpose?) of getting into the vicar's good books, thereby guaranteeing access to the school with church affiliation. Other schools have a requirement to live in catchment, an area usually mapped with extreme accuracy and precision; living on the other side of the road may be outside the domain. Some parents are reduced to moving house or giving a false address – grandma's for example – if it means their 'choice' can be realised.

In addition to the uncertainty about the status or category of school in which our young people should be educated, there is also some lack of clarity over what it is that schools are actually there to achieve. Alongside any argument about school placement must surely come discussion about what education – in whatever establishment – is actually meant to accomplish. From time to time teachers, and perhaps especially headteachers, will question their philosophy of education, the aims of their school and – particularly after a bad day – wonder what the point of it all is. There are naturally many views about the prime purpose of schooling, and debate has filled countless books and journals. One prevailing opinion sees school essentially as preparation for adult and working life. *The Children's Plan*, a consultation paper published in 2008 by the Department for Children, Schools and Families, had an opening paragraph which stated that *'schools rightly see their central purpose as preparing children and young people for life.'* This of course is extremely important, particularly if such preparation involves providing appropriate opportunities for students to acquire relevant qualifications and skills. More questionable though is another view put forward by the Prime Minister and his Deputy in the November 2010 White Paper, *The Importance of Teaching*. This document opens with a paragraph saying that what really matters is how the country compares with our international competitors. Back to league tables again!

However laudable these aims – who would deny the importance of young people becoming well qualified, for example? – it has always seemed to me that coming top of the Nations' League or, more importantly, preparing young people for adulthood, can only be a part of the equation. As described in a previous chapter, Henry Morris expounded passionately the belief that school should be about so much more than this. Current political thinking has appeared to promote the idea of an educational end-product – and the need to compete on the world's stage – above any notion that education might conceivably be of value in its own right.

Ted Wragg used to warn his trainee teachers that everyone was a self-appointed expert on education. Many people, it appears, are able to voice strong opinion and say exactly what is wrong with the country's schools. The media have had a field day with this. But what exactly *is* wrong? There is a school (sorry) of thought that wishes the nation's educational establishments simply to replicate bygone tradition; a desire to drive with a constant focus on the rear-view mirror rather than on the road ahead. Yes, certainly heads must ensure that high standards are upheld, but they do not want the kind of education policy driven by hindsight or back-to-basics nonsense. I have often been struck by the hypocrisy of some of this claptrap: politicians, for example, pronouncing on the moral values that schools should promote whilst having extra-marital relationships and claiming expenses to which they are not entitled.

After all the initiatives and reforms of the past twenty or so years – National Curriculum, Ofsted, published league tables and testing students to destruction – are our children really any better off? Are they now happier? Do they enjoy school more? Evidence would suggest not. Are they more fulfilled as individuals? Hard to say. Or more socially or spiritually rich? Pass. And does Whitehall or Westminster really know best? We have been continually subjected to a diet of simplistic, quick-fix solutions imparted from central government. Pull the lever in Whitehall and the resulting action will be enabled in every classroom in the land. Problem with obesity? Simple, introduce a programme of healthy eating into schools – job done. The level of salt in children's diet was regarded as an issue a few years back. Solution: ban salt-cellars on tables in school dining rooms – box ticked. Let's teach about the sanctity of marriage: that came from a government whose leader, the Prime Minister, had a four-year affair with a former member of his Cabinet – out of the Cabinet into the closet. Clause 28 was another cause-celèbre, when the government's view of homosexuality was trapped in the era of Oscar Wilde. This pernicious piece of legislation, in place from 1998 to 2003 – in Scotland it was repealed earlier – forbade schools from any form of promotion of homosexuality or gay family relationships. No wonder MP's who were gay were reticent about coming out. Now, fortunately, we live in more enlightened times: politicians freely come out of the closet and into the Cabinet.

But all this direction from on high has had limited effect. Control from the top is an imprecise science; giraffes are not very good at tying their own shoelaces. The search for a definitive solution to the 'problem' of what needs to be done about our schools goes on, just like the search for a unified theory of the universe, where general relativity and quantum mechanics are at one. Where is education's Higgs Boson? Is there a panacea or some kind of unifying theory for education? Or are we are searching for something that simply doesn't exist?

In1887 Albert Michelson and Edward Morely, two American physicists, conducted an experiment to measure the motion of the Earth relative to the aether. The aether was imagined to be an all-pervading, weightless and invisible fluid which occupied every corner of the universe. Its presence was thought to be essential as a medium through which light could travel… sound waves require air (you will recall)… light waves required the aether. As an experiment it failed spectacularly. The motion of the Earth through this fluid with such remarkably intangible properties could not be measured. And why could it not be measured? Because the aether did not exist! As a result, 19th century physics theory was thrown back into the melting pot, paving the way for

CHAPTER 25

Walking the Dog

Just like any established member of the family, a dog gives the pleasure of unconditional affection, attentive companionship and endless support. A dog never disagrees with you, doesn't challenge your judgement and is unfailingly loyal. My black labrador, a faithful four-legged friend, listens patiently to all I say to him without ever voicing criticism. He never judges me, nor shows any hint of impatience or annoyance, and has kept every secret he has ever been told. He – and before him, an equally lovable golden retriever – has been at my side for the years of my headship, on countless walks during which I have sought, and found, inspiration for all manner of school-related issues and strategies. Forward planning for meetings, staff-training sessions and assemblies; long term projects and shorter term developments – many have been conceived, contemplated and refined during these walks. My constant companion has never once dismissed a bright idea of mine or sought to counter an opinion, worrying only about when the next stick would be thrown or whether I still had biscuits in my pocket. He has also helped me through the manifold problems and difficulties such as beset headteachers from time to time throughout their careers. Together we have walked the paths and fields near my home almost every weekend in term-time and nearly every day in school holidays.

And now, in retirement, I have more time to enjoy the rambles with my devoted dog and have the opportunity to reflect on my career as a headteacher. Today it is a Monday morning in January – and I am not at school. The first real week of my retirement finds me walking with my canine chum who, it appears, is as appreciative of my newly-found status as I am. There is no long car journey with its frustrations of traffic jams and hold-ups; I have swapped the motorway for the fields, the tarmac for the grass, and the stress of the road for the tranquillity of the countryside. As we walk, I might be tempted to dwell upon the many controversial aspects of headship I have endured, the frustrations of the ceaseless change for change's sake, and the relentlessly increasing politicisation of education. But enough of all that for now. And in any case, none of these annoyances – exasperating as at times they were – could ever really detract from the immense joy, pride and satisfaction I have experienced throughout my time as a headteacher.

A quick calculation suggests that, over the course of my career, I have taught, and been responsible for, many thousands of young people who have gone on to become doctors, teachers, business men and women, or found success in other occupations, trades and professions. There have also been two league footballers, an international triathlete, a famous comedian and TV celebrity, the daughter of a sixties rock-and-roll singer and a page three pin-up girl – so many wonderful characters, who I sincerely hope will have benefited to some degree from my influence as a teacher and a head.

As I pass through the gate which leads through a small thicket, and cross the stream into open countryside, I think back to the students who arrived into my care fresh from primary school, then very much still children. My school had been well known – justifiably in my opinion – for its annual Primary Week, when students due to join the school in September spent five full days with us shortly before the end of the previous term. Nearly two hundred 11-year olds from three main feeder primaries, and a number of other schools in the county, spent the week following a full secondary-school timetable. They were placed in their new groups where they met their form tutor and head of year. Hours of planning were expended in making the week the success it always was. In all my time as headteacher I never discovered another school which offered such an induction. Most had a 'transition' day or two but none gave such a comprehensive introduction to secondary school as we did.

Five years later, as young adults, students left to take up places at sixth form or further education college. I recall the annual leavers' ball to which students – in full evening dress – arrived at school in a manner of styles and by all means of transport; a competition to outdo each other had been in place for years. Stretch limousines were once an extremely novel and stylish way to arrive but eventually became ten-a-penny. More recently we saw students pitch up in vintage cars, tractors, horse and cart, even a fire-engine and a London Transport double-decker bus. I sometimes found myself wondering where it would all end. Micro-light aircraft and helicopters? No one had yet thought of arriving by hot air balloon, but I suppose it may happen. This was always one of the evenings to savour. No inspectors; no policy documents or forms to complete; no agendas or minutes of the last meeting: just an opportunity to celebrate students' successful conclusion to five years of secondary education.

And what about the staff? So many conscientious and hard working teachers, classroom assistants, administrative, reception, site and finance staff who made my school what it was. These loyal colleagues fulfilled their various roles superbly as part of a successful team. The whole functioning more than the sum of the parts – just like the energy in an atomic nucleus. But enough too of physics. As might be expected, there were a few mavericks and the occasional character who, for whatever reason, chose not to engage with our ethos. Some moved on to other schools more to their liking and, over the years, a handful of individuals – perhaps wisely – decided to leave the profession. But most – the vast majority – liked the school enough to want to stay.

As I reach the small river where my dog likes to swim, I am persuaded to throw a stick for him to retrieve, endeavouring to stay dry as he places the recovered article in front of me and shakes his coat vigorously. I shudder to think what temperature the water must be but he seems not to mind in the slightest. He would leap in and out all day if allowed.

I remember the hours spent each year as Christmas approached, with the need to find inspiration for my end of term speech delivered to the staff at their Christmas lunch. This event had become a very strong tradition – thoroughly enjoyed, I was always told, and anticipated with relish. There were usually staff to whom we said farewell; sometimes, for those most long-serving colleagues, this was accomplished by means of a specially written song – something else created on my weekend walks. I usually persuaded my deputies to join me in making fools of ourselves. I sometimes feared though that I was prone to taking things a little too far. The end of term Christmas speech, which I had started as a means of bringing a little light relief to staff at the end of a busy term, became a self-inflicted burden. My deputies often feigned reluctance, but I was convinced that they secretly enjoyed the variety of immature behaviour, more fitting for the stage than the staff room. Over the years, the end of term celebrations involved 'appearances' by Elton John, the Beatles and – most famously – Dame Edna Everage who arrived to give a farewell to a teacher about to depart for a year's secondment down-under. I was constantly asked to repeat this performance but, in my view, dressing up in drag is something – like a triathlon – which is best not repeated.

Schools are unique places to work and learn. With trust and

confidence in each other, I have seen staff provide outstanding education and care for our young people. I was proud to have played my part in leading a school which always placed great emphasis on the all-round, Henry Morris ideal of education: education which seeks to promote and develop the intellectual and social growth of the students in our care; education where academic success and exam results are important but do not eclipse everything else; education which is more than simply a means to an end. It has been a privilege to see students' pride in performing in concert or on stage; their participation in sport; their successful completion of a community service or work experience placement; the team work; the successes and the near misses; the excitement and love of a particular subject; and the friends and relationships which have lasted beyond school.

My final days were awash with emotion. There were cards, presents, speeches and the naming of a suite of new rooms in my honour. I was genuinely humbled by the sincerity and generosity of all my colleagues. There was a musical rap, written by my deputies – at last getting something of their own back on me – in which every member of staff took part.

We are away from the river now and walking up the byway through a small wood which leads to the main path homeward. The trees are almost bare, the path is strewn with leaves and the ground underfoot remains sodden from the previous day's rain. My dog indicates his desire for me to throw his stick again by placing it at my feet, backing away and lying down in anticipation of the next chase. Would he ever tire of this activity? It seems unlikely. He has simple needs: food and water, a comfortable bed and the love and affection of his family. And though it could hardly be described as a need, he does seem to so enjoy the endless chasing of a well-thrown stick. And who am I to deny him that?

As I turn finally for home, I find myself contemplating my newly-found state of retirement with an almost equal mixture of excitement and sadness. Excitement at the prospect of time for the many activities I enjoy and in which I am now more able to indulge; sadness at having left so many wonderful colleagues and friends, and the school which has been so much part of my life for almost a quarter of a century. As we reach home, I cannot avoid looking at my watch to imagine what would be happening were I at school. Morning briefing has now finished, assembly too. There will be various meetings throughout the day, parents and staff to see, a class to teach, then bus duty and a parents' evening later. I wrest myself away from such thoughts and consider instead how I will fill my days ahead, away from the pressures of school. Not too difficult I conclude; undoubtedly there is life after headship, and much to keep me occupied.

And in the meantime I have a book to write.

Acknowledgements

Morris, H., *The Village College: Being a memorandum on the Provision of Educational and Social Facilities for the Countryside, with Special References to Cambridgeshire,* (1924), Morris: Cambridge.

Orwell, G., *Nineteen Eighty-Four* (1968), Penguin: Middlesex.